WRITING THROUGH EARLY MODERN HISTORY

Level 2
"Cursive Models"

A Charlotte Mason Writing Program
"Gentle and Complete"

Early Modern History
1600-1850
From Captain John Smith to the California Gold Rush

Historical Narratives, Primary Source Documents, Poetry, and Cultural Tales

BOOKS PUBLISHED BY BROOKDALE HOUSE:

The Writing Through Ancient History books
Writing Through Ancient History Level 1 Cursive Models
Writing Through Ancient History Level 1 Manuscript Models
Writing Through Ancient History Level 2 Cursive Models
Writing Through Ancient History Level 2 Manuscript Models

The Writing Through Medieval History books
Writing Through Medieval History Level 1 Cursive Models
Writing Through Medieval History Level 1 Manuscript Models
Writing Through Medieval History Level 2 Cursive Models
Writing Through Medieval History Level 2 Manuscript Models

The Writing Through Early Modern History Books
Writing Through Early Modern History Level 1 Cursive Models
Writing Through Early Modern History Level 1 Manuscript Models
Writing Through Early Modern History Level 2 Cursive Models
Writing Through Early Modern History Level 2 Manuscript Models

The Writing Through Modern History Books
Writing Through Modern History Level 1 Cursive Models
Writing Through Modern History Level 1 Manuscript Models
Writing Through Modern History Level 2 Cursive Models
Writing Through Modern History Level 2 Manuscript Models

The Fun Spanish Level 1

Sheldon's Primary Language Lessons
(Introductory grammar workbook for elementary students)

The Westminster Shorter Catechism Copybook
(Available in the following font styles: traditional, modern, italic, and vertical, both print and cursive)

The Geography Drawing Series
Drawing Around the World: Europe
Drawing Around the World: USA

Easy Narrative Writing

ISBN: 978-1-64281-036-3

© Copyright 2015. Kimberly Garcia. Published by Brookdale House. Brookdale House grants permission to photocopy pages for use within a single family. All other rights reserved. For permission to make copies, written or otherwise, except for the use within one immediate family, please contact the author at www.brookdalehouse.com or Kimberly@brookdalehouse.com .

Table of Contents

Introduction		v
Definitions—Narration, Copywork, Studied Dictation		vii
Scheduling		x

Chapter I

Captain John Smith	(1580-1631)*	I-3
A White Boy among the Indians, about Virginia Colony	(1609)	I-9
The Pine-Tree Shillings, about currency in the colonies	(1652)	I-13
Sir Isaac Newton, about childhood	(1642-1727)	I-18
King Philip to the White Settler	(1675-1676)	I-23
King Charles II and William Penn, about Pennsylvania	(1681)	I-28
The Whistle by Benjamin Franklin, about childhood	(1712)	I-34
Young Benjamin Franklin, by Nathaniel Hawthorne	(1716)	I-38
Little Lord Sold into Bondage, about European slavery	(1743)	I-43
The Story of Peter Williamson—Twice a Slave	(1745)	I-48
The Intrepid Youth, about George Washington	(1750)	I-52
Franklin's Wonderful Kite, by James Baldwin	(1752)	I-58
Grandmother Bear, about Indian culture	(1763-1766)	I-63
The Good Reader, about Frederick the Great, King of Prussia	(1712-1786)	I-68
Boston Tea Party	(1773)	I-73
The Midnight Ride, about Paul Revere	(1775)	I-77
The Young Scout, about Andrew Jackson	(1780)	I-82
Elizabeth Zane, about time of Revolutionary War	(1777-1782)	I-86
The Capture of Major Andre, about Benedict Arnold	(1780)	I-91
Webster and the Woodchuck, about Daniel Webster	(1792)	I-96
Benedict Arnold, references Reign of Terror	(1793)	I-101
Old Johnny Appleseed	(1774-1845)	I-106
Napoleon's Army Crossing the Alps	(1800)	I-111
A Foot Race for Life, about Lewis and Clark Expedition	(1804-1806)	I-115
The Rescue, about rescue out on the open sea	(1831)	I-120
The Whisperers, about Elihu Burritt, social activist	(1810-1879)	I-125
Finding Gold in California	(1849)	I-130

Chapter II

The Mayflower Compact	(1620)	II-3
Benjamin Franklin's 13 Virtues, from autobiography	(1706-1790)	II-6
Give Me Liberty or Give Me Death, by Patrick Henry	(1775)	II-9
Common Sense by Thomas Paine, excerpt	(1776)	II-13
The Declaration of Independence, excerpt	(1776)	II-17
Preamble to The Constitution	(1787)	II-22
A Letter to James Madison, by Thomas Jefferson excerpt	(1787)	II-25
The United States Bill of Rights, original ten	(1789)	II-28

*Note: Dates denote the year of the story or the life span of the central figure or event.

Proclamation of A National Thanksgiving	(1789)	II-32
George Washington's Farewell Address excerpt	(1796)	II-35
Jefferson's Letter to the Danbury Baptists	(1802)	II-38
President Andrew Jackson on Indian Removal excerpt	(1830)	II-41
Life of Tecumseh excerpt	(1841)	II-45
Life and Adventures of Black Hawk excerpt	(1843)	II-48
A Slave Narrative excerpt, by himself, Henry Bibb	(1849)	II-52
On the Duty of Civil Disobedience excerpt by Henry David Thoreau	(1849)	II-55

Chapter III

America, by Samuel Francis Smith	(1831)**	III-3
The Anti-Slavery Alphabet (fragment), by Anonymous	(1847)	III-6
A Book of Nonsense excerpt, by Edward Lear	(1846)	III-9
The First Thanksgiving, by Margaret Junkin Preston	(1820-1807)	III-12
Hiawatha, by Henry Wadsworth Longfellow	(1855)	III-16
The Landing of the Pilgrims, by Felicia Hemans	(1830)	III-21
The Little Boy Lost / Found, by William Blake	(1789)	III-25
Love Between Brothers and Sisters, by Isaac Watts	(1877)	III-28
On a Circle / Vowels, by Jonathan Swift	(1667-1745)***	III-31
Paul Revere's Ride, by Henry Wadsworth Longfellow	(1860)	III-34
The Star-Spangled Banner, by Francis Scott Key	(1814)	III-39
Woodman, Spare That Tree, by George P. Morris	(1830)	III-42

Chapter IV+

A Blackfoot Story, an Indian Tale		IV-3
Hans, Who Made the Princess Laugh, a Norwegian Tale		IV-8
The Horse That Aroused the Town an Italian Folktale		IV-14
Mother Holle, a German Folktale	(1812-1815)	IV-19
The Old Man and His Grandson, a German Folktale	(1812-1815)	IV-25
Snow-White and Rose-Red, a German Folktale	(1812-1815	IV-29
The Three Tasks, by the Brothers Grimm	(1812-1815)	IV-36
Why the Sea Is Salt, a Norse Tale		IV-41

Appendix

Oral narration questions	2
Grammar Guide	3
Models from Chapter I Historical Narratives	6
Models from Chapter II Text Excerpts from Primary Source Documents	14
Models from Chapter III Poetry from Early Modern History	19
Models from Chapter IV Folktales from Various Cultures	25

**Note: Because the time of historical relevance does not match the date of publication, the poetry selections are in alphabetical order.
***Note: The publication was not available for the author's work, the life span of the author is indicated.
+Note: Not all of the publication dates for Chapter IV are included. These are very old tales with many variations published at various times.

Introduction

Writing Through Early Modern History Layout

Writing Through Early Modern History is a writing program that teaches grammar, spelling, and history—all at once. This volume covers early modern history, from 1600 AD to 1850 AD—the third year of a 4-year cycle.

Writing Through Early Modern History, L2 teaches writing the Charlotte Mason way for upper grammar stage students, third through fifth grade. It is divided into four chapters: short stories, text excerpts from primary source documents, poetry, and cultural tales. For Chapter I, short stories that give insight into people, places, and events during early modern times have been selected. Chapter II contains excerpts from primary source documents including, but not limited to, historical essays, personal letters and government documents from the establishment and development of America. Chapter III contains poetry from and about early modern times. Chapter IV contains folk tales.

In all four chapters, the reading selection is followed by a practice model, which is used for copywork and dictation. There are more than 60 selections included in *Writing Through Early Modern History*.

To coordinate *Writing Through Early Modern History* with your history topics, refer to the Table of Contents, which also serves as a timeline. Use the timeline provided to determine which selection would be the best fit for that week's history lesson. Historical narratives will primarily come from Chapters I and IV. Feel free to move around the book.

In the Appendix, you will find two models for each reading selection. The first model is the same as the copywork model which followed the reading selection. The second model, which is in italics, is also from the reading selection. It has been added for use by those that like to use a separate model for dictation.

Because *Writing Through Early Modern History* was written for grades 3–5, some selections will be too long for some students. Simply reduce any of the models by drawing a line through the unneeded portion. Sometimes you will have to break the model in the middle of a sentence. In that case, stop at a semi-colon (;) or coordinating conjunction (", and" ", or" ", but" ", nor" ", for" ", so" ", yet") to make the selection shorter. Semi-colons and coordinating conjunctions are used to separate main clauses—those with a subject and a predicate. If you must break the model into a shorter sentence, modify the new selection by adding a period at the end and ensure that you have a grammatically correct model. Explain to your student the use of semi-colons and coordinating conjunctions and why the change is being made. This is an excellent opportunity to reinforce and explain the grammar rules involved.

Note: Many of the works included were taken from the public domain; many have been edited for Writing Through Early Modern History.

Note: Although titles of books and ships would normally be italicized in texts, they are underlined to teach children that these names are underlined in handwritten works.

Most of the principles in *Writing Through Early Modern History* are based on the work of Ms. Charlotte Mason. She advocated that children of the grammar or elementary stage practice narration, copywork, and dictation as their primary method of learning to write. But because Ms. Mason's methods have been interpreted differently over the years, I have included alternative suggestions on how to implement *Writing Through Early Modern History*. So to begin using *Writing Through Early Modern History* as your child's writing program, please read all of the introduction, pages v–ix, before your student begins.

Additional Information

Reading Levels
Chapters II and III contain excerpts from historical documents and historically relevant poetry that may be well above the reading level of some grammar and even logic stage students. I recommend that these advanced selections be read to your student. If you would like to stretch your student, ask him to read all or part of the selection back to you. These reading selections offer great opportunity to cover new vocabulary as well as new ideas.

Appendix "Models Only"
The Appendix lists all of the models by chapter. The first model is in normal typeface while the second model is italicized. Only the first model follows the reading selections. The second models were added to give the students a different model for dictation. For the sake of organization, the Appendix contains a copy of the models to assist the instructor with copywork and studied dictation.

Getting Started
On the following page, I have covered each area of the program: Narration, Copywork, and Dictation. I have also provided a guide suggesting how to incorporate grammar into the program. Please read these in their entirety.

Correcting Work
Correcting writing, whether written summations, copywork, or dictation, is always difficult. Ms. Mason advised teachers and parents to correct the student's writings occasionally. This makes perfect sense when realizing that Ms. Mason's methods did not require the need for extensive corrections. She consistently emphasized that work be done correctly the first time. She believed that a student should not be allowed to visually dwell on incorrect work. When a child made a mistake during dictation, Ms. Mason had stamps or pieces of paper available to cover the mistakes so that the mistakes were not reinforced visually.

When a child made a mistake during narrations, she withheld correcting him. I believe that she used the time after the oral narration was finished to discuss the material that had been narrated. When corrections are needed, it is good to practice the principle of praise before correcting children. Find out what is right with what they've done. Be impressed. Focus on their effort. Build them up. Ephesians 5:29 of the King James Bible says—

Let no corrupt communication
proceed out of your mouth, but
that which is good to the use of edifying,
that it may minister grace
unto the hearers.

A Note on a CulturalTerm
Throughout this text, you will find the word *Indian* used in reference to Native Americans. The reason for this is two-fold. First, many of the stories used in this text were written at a time when the term *Indian* was commonly used to refer to those peoples that are now known as the First Americans. Second, the modern term—*Native American*—has not been and is not fully accepted by most people that are known as *Native Americans*. Because there is no one term that has been fully agreed upon and because the word *Indian* is not deemed derogatory but outdated, the original word *Indian* is used throughout this text. By leaving this term in place, instructors are giving an opportunity to discuss, with their students, how this term has been used and viewed throughout history, and how this term is being used, and is currently viewed, in today's modern times.

Definitions
Personal Narrations –the act of retelling

Ms. Mason believed narrations should be done immediately after the story was read to the student or by the student. Narrations are very simple, yet very effective in teaching writing. The act of narrating helps children to internalize the content of the reading material they have been exposed to and allows them to make it their own. In order to narrate, students must listen carefully, dissect the information, and then express that same information in their own words. It is a powerful tool, but very simple to put into practice.

Oral narrations Read all or part of the story only once before requiring the student to narrate! It will require him to pay attention. Simply ask your student to tell you what he has just heard or read.

If your student has trouble with this process, show him how to narrate by demonstrating the process for him. **Read a selection yourself and then narrate it to him. Ask him to imitate you.** If he continues to draw a blank, use the list of questions below to prompt him. (See the removable list of narration questions in the Appendix, page 2, for daily use. The Appendix also contains questions for poetry and primary source documents.)

Besides all of the previously mentioned benefits, oral narrations teach students to digest information, dissect it, and reorganize it into their own words while thinking on their feet. This practice helps students to develop the art of public speaking. This formal process will force them to express their ideas without a written plan. It strengthens the mind. And over time, their speech will become fluent and natural. (I sometimes have my children stand as they narrate. It makes the process more formal.)

If your student has difficulty with narrations, ask some or all of the following questions:

1. Who was the main character?
2. What was the character like?
3. Where was the character?
4. What time was it in the story?
5. Who else was in the story?
6. Does the main character have an enemy?
   (The enemy may be another character, himself, or nature.)
7. Did the main character have a problem? If not, what did the character want?
8. What does the main character do? What does he say? If there are others, what do they do?
9. Why does the character do what he does?
10. What happens to the character as he tries to solve his problem?
11. Is there a moral to the story? If so, what was it?
12. What happens at the end of the story? Or how does the main character finally solve his problem?

Written Summations Around the age of 10, students were required by Ms. Mason to write down their narrations for themselves. Many students can do this earlier. Written summations will allow your student to develop this skill. If your student is able, have him write as much as he can, as perfectly as he can, even around the age of 8.

At the end of each oral narration, ask your child to summarize the reading selection by identifying the beginning, the middle, and the end. He should be able to do this in about three to six sentences—fewer is best. Younger students will sometimes begin each sentence with "First,..." or "At the beginning,..." This is okay. But once the student masters the summation, ask him to summarize without these types of words. Tell him to begin with the subject or the time.

Ex: When Louisa May Alcott was a young girl, she was very happy because she spent her time playing with her sisters and writing in her diary.

The benefits of written summations are manifold. They will help your student to think linearly from the beginning of the reading selection to the end. They also provide the right amount of content for the reluctant writer. Additionally, the act of summarizing teaches students to identify the main thread or central idea of a passage. (Even though your child begins to write his written summations, have him continue his oral narrations without limit. These will help him to internalize and learn the historical content of the stories in *Writing Through Early Modern History* as well as develop his public speaking skills.)

Copywork and Grammar—copying a passage exactly as written

As your child copies the model before him, stay near so that you are able to correct any problems immediately.

Before your child begins, discuss the model with him. Point out the grammatical elements that he is learning. Have your child identify the part of speech in the model and circle it with a colored pencil. See page 3 of the Appendix for a grammar guide. (Spend approximately one month on each new part of speech.) When using the grammar guide, continue to review by including all previously learned work in the current lesson. For the second month, he is to identify both nouns and verbs. The third—nouns, verbs, and pronouns.

Ms. Mason recommended the formal study of grammar at about 4th or 5th grade. If you opt to add a formal program for your upper grammar stage student, that would be worthwhile. If you do so, you may omit the grammar study in this program.

Grammar
If you would prefer that your student study grammar with his copywork, see the grammar guide in the Appendix page 3. It focuses on the 8 parts of speech as well as fundamental punctuation. The process involves the student identifying the parts of speech and color-coding the copywork selections according to the guide. The process is cumulative in that students should roll the new grammar concept in with the old. By of the end of the year, students should be identifying all eight parts of speech in their copywork.

Studied Dictation—the act of writing from an oral reading

Once again, Ms. Mason's ideas are simple, yet effective. The goal in dictation is to teach your child to write correctly and from memory the sentences or clauses he has just heard. Ms. Mason let the child study the dictation for a few minutes. She wrote down any unknown or difficult words for him on a board. She then erased the board and read each passage only once. From this one reading, the child wrote; however, if the child made a mistake, she covered the mistake instantly so that the student was not allowed to visualize and internalize it.

For the child who has never done dictation, start by reading as many times as necessary so that your child memorizes the sentences. Work down to one reading per 2 or 3 sentences or main clauses. This is an advanced skill and may require time to achieve. Be patient, but consistent. (If needed, allow your student to repeat the model back to you before he writes. Some students may need this reinforcement; others may not.)

After you write the model on the whiteboard, discuss it, in depth, with your student. An example of the process follows.

MODEL

"Mary, did you spill the ink on the carpet?" asked Tom.
"No, Tom," answered Mary. "Did you, Will?"
"I did not, Mary, but I know who did," said Will.
"Who was it, Will?"

Will did not answer in words. He pointed a finger at Fido, and guilty little Fido crept under the sofa.

QUESTIONS TO ASK:

1. What are the names of the people in this story? How does each name begin?
    The names of people always begin with capital letters.
2. Study this model, telling what words begin with capitals and why; which words are indented and why; what marks of punctuation are used and why.

FIRST PARAGRAPH

3. Why is Mary indented in this paragraph.
4. Why is Mary capitalized? Why are the names capitalized?
5. Why is there a comma to separate "Mary" from the rest of the sentence?
6. Why are there quotation marks around certain words?
7. Why does the quoted sentence end with a question mark?
8. Why do some sentences end with a period?

SECOND PARAGRAPH

9. Where does the second paragraph begin?
10. The paragraph begins with someone speaking. How do we know this?
11. Why is the word no capitalized?
12. Why is there a comma after no?
13. Why is there a comma after Tom? After you?
14. Why is there a period after Mary and a question after Will.

DO THIS WITH EACH PARAGRAPH

If there are any questions that your student cannot answer, tell him the answers. Discuss the grammar with him, and work with him until he can narrate why the model is punctuated the way it is.

Do the same with spelling. Identify the words that your student doesn't know and discuss why that word is spelled the way it is.

To see an example of studied dictation, visit the youtube video at the link below:
https://www.youtube.com/watch?v=xoTACGomwsw

or search "Studied Dictation Demonstration" on youtube.
There I demonstrate this dictation process.

Scheduling Information

Listed below is a recommendation for the use of *Writing Through Early Modern History*; however, this is **only a recommendation** and should be adjusted for your student's individual needs. **Further explanations and alternate methods** are included on the next page. Please feel free to adjust these methods to make writing as painless as possible for your student. Every child is different.

One Suggested Schedule:

Day 1 — **Reading, Oral Narrations, and Written Summations**
From the Table of Contents, choose a story from Chapters I or IV.
Either you or your student should read the story selection once.
First, have the student orally narrate the story back to you.
(If he has difficulty, use the narration questions listed in the Appendix.)
Second, ask the student to summarize the story in about three sentences to six sentences. If he is able, have him write one or more sentences from his summation. Write for him, if needed. **(For more on narrations, see page vii.)**

Day 2 — **Copywork and Grammar** Complete Model Practice 1 from Day 1's reading selection. Discuss/explain the grammar and punctuation in the model. Do a color-coded grammar study.
(For more on copywork and grammar, see page viii.)

Day 3 — **Studied Dictation** Complete Model Practice 2, using the additional model located in the Appendix, also from Day 1's reading selection. Follow the guidelines for studied dictation on page viii. Neatly write the italic model provided in the Appendix for your student on a separate paper or white board. Allow the student to study the model before writing. Erase the model and dictate.

Day 4 — **Oral narrations and Copywork**
From the Table of Contents, choose a selection from Chapters II or III.
Read all **or part** of the primary source document to your student. He may read the poem himself. If so, teach him to read with expression.
Discuss the complicated ideas in the document. Have your student narrate what he has learned. Complete Model Practice 1 using the copywork model.

Day 5 — **Studied Dictation** Complete Model Practice 2, also from Day 4's reading selection. Follow the guidelines for studied dictation on page viii. Neatly write the Italic model provided in the Appendix for your student on a separate piece of paper or a white board. Allow the student to study the model before writing. Erase the model and dictate.

If the models are too long

If the models are too long for your student, reduce them. Third graders, or even older reluctant writers, should not be forced to do more than they are able. See the bold paragraph on page v for guidelines on reducing the models.

If your child isn't ready for dictation

Replace the dictation with copywork of the same model, or write the dictation model from the Appendix into the model practice 2 area. Have your student copy your written model in the model practice 3 area.

Optional Schedules

Charlotte Mason's Methods

Ms. Mason used narration, copywork, and dictation simultaneously throughout a young child's education. Narrations were done immediately after he had listened to or read the selection. Copywork was done from well-written sentences. And while many don't believe copywork to be valuable once a student learns to write from dictation, Ms. Mason believed that copywork was extremely valuable for many years alongside dictation. Dictation was a separate part of the process, mostly for the purpose of teaching spelling.

Ms. Mason allowed students to look at the dictation passages and study them before the student began writing. This process was helpful because it allowed the student to visualize how the passage should look. It taught him to study with intention. It taught him to focus on the words. After the passage was read once, the student wrote the passage from memory. This method improved a child's spelling and his grasp of correct punctuation as well.

But not everyone who follows Ms. Mason's methods follows each area of narration, copywork, and dictation in the same way. Below are some ways to incorporate some or all of these ideas into your child's learning adventure.

Different Copywork Passages Daily

Simply use *Writing Through Early Modern History* as written, covering two stories per week. **Day 1**, pick a selection from Chapters I or IV. Read and have the student do an oral narration and a written summation. **Day 2**, do copywork and a color-coded grammar study of the model. **Day 3**, the teacher should write all or part of the italicized model from the Appendix onto the Model Practice 2 area, in ink. The student should copy the model and then do a color-coded grammar study of the model in the Model Practice 2 area. **Day 4**, pick a selection from Chapters II or III, a primary source selection or poetry selection. Do oral narration, copywork, and a color-coded grammar study of the model. **Day 5**, the teacher should write the italicized model from the Appendix onto the Model Practice 2 area, in ink. The student should copy the model and do a color-coded grammar study of the model in the Model Practice 2 area. This will provide your student with four different copywork selections each week from two different sources.

Copywork as Dictation

Day 1, pick a selection from Chapters I or IV. Read and have the student do an oral narration and a written summation. **Day 2**, do copywork and a color-coded grammar study of the model. **Day 3**, do studied dictation of the same model. Have your student write in the Model Practice 2 area. **Day 4**, pick a selection from Chapters II or III, a primary source selection or poetry selection. Do an oral narration, copywork, and a color-coded grammar study of the model. **Day 5**, do a studied dictation of yesterday's copywork. Have your student write in the Model Practice 2 area.

Copywork and Dictation

Follow the suggested schedule on page x.

Reminders and Helps

- Use *Writing Through Early Modern History* in the best way possible to serve your student's needs. Adapt any area as necessary.
- Help students with spelling as necessary. Set your student up for success.
- In the case of dialogue, remind your student that each time a different character is speaking, a new paragraph is started via indentions. When he first encounters this, show him an example before requiring it of him.
- If the size of the selection is too large, **simply reduce it and require less.**
- Set your student up for success. He shouldn't be expected to know what he has not yet been taught.
- To sum up Charlotte Mason's methods:

Quality over quantity.
Accuracy over speed.
Ideas over drill.
Perfection over mediocrity.

Added Note on Paragraphing
For full-length written narrations (not summations, but the whole story)

You may want your student to occasionally write his narrations in place of the summation. Ms. Mason had children begin writing their narrations around the age of 10. This is equivalent to fourth or fifth grade, and it is a good time for most students. To make the transition to written narrations, have your student orally narrate first, then ask him to write down his narration. Eventually he won't need the oral narration.

In the actual writing of the narration, the difficult elements for most students will be punctuation, grammar, spelling, and paragraph breaks. Through the copywork and dictation, students actively learn correct punctuation, grammar, and spelling. And although they make mistakes, with practice in these areas, they will improve.

Paragraph breaks, however, are not often taught—in any curriculum. Many students intuitively learn when to begin a new paragraph because they read well-written literature. But this isn't always enough.

Paragraphing is easy to learn. Each time the who, what, when, where, why, or how of the story changes, a new paragraph is begun. Look at the following story—

The Penny-Wise Monkey
re-told by Ellen C. Babbitt
from More Jataka Tales

  Once upon a time the king of a large and rich country gathered together his army to take a faraway little country. The king and his soldiers marched all morning long and then went into camp in the forest.
(who=king and soldiers, what=march and went, when=once upon a time, where=camp in forest, why=to take a country)

  When they fed the horses, they gave them some peas to eat. One of the Monkeys living in the forest saw the peas and jumped down to get some of them. He filled his mouth and hands with them, and up into the tree he went again, and sat down to eat the peas.
(New paragraph, a change in the what, what=gave the horses peas, change in the when, when=feeding the horses, the monkey is introduced)

xii

As he sat there eating the peas, one pea fell from his hand to the ground. At once, the greedy Monkey dropped all the peas he had in his hands and ran down to hunt for the lost pea. But he could not find that one pea. He climbed up into his tree again and sat still looking very glum. "To get more, I threw away what I had," he said to himself.
(New paragraph, a change in the who, the story is now focused on the monkey and not the king, who=monkey)

The king had watched the Monkey, and he said to himself, "I will not be like this foolish Monkey, who lost much to gain a little. I will go back to my own country and enjoy what I now have."
(New paragraph, a change in the who, who=the king, the story is now focused on the king again)

So he and his men marched back home.
(New paragraph, a change in the what, what=marched back home)

Also, when writing dialogue in a conversation, a new paragraph is started each time a different character is speaking.

Bonus Materials

To learn of new publications and free educational resources, sign up for our newsletter at

www.brookdalehouse.com

or

scan:

CHAPTER I

Historical Narratives Covering Early Modern History

Captain John Smith
by Richard G. Parker

The adventures of this singular man are so various, and so very extraordinary, that the detail of them seems more like romance than true history. He was born in Lincolnshire, England, and was left an orphan at an early age.

His love of adventure displayed itself while he was yet a schoolboy. He sold his satchel, books and clothes, and went over to France, without the knowledge of his guardians.

Afterward, he served as a soldier in the Netherlands for several years. At the end of his campaign, he returned to England, where he recovered a small portion of the estate left him by his deceased father.

At the age of seventeen, this money enabled him to resume his travels under more favorable auspices. He again went to France and embarked at Marseilles, with some pious pilgrims, bound to Italy.

During this voyage a violent tempest threatened destruction to the vessel; and poor Smith being the suspected cause of the impending danger was thrown, without mercy, into the sea.

He saved himself by his expertness in swimming; and soon after he boarded another vessel, bound to Alexandria, where he entered into the service of the Emperor of Austria, against the Turks.

His bravery, and great ingenuity in all the stratagems of war, soon made him famous and obtained for him the command of two hundred and fifty horsemen.

At the siege of Regal, the Ottomans sent a challenge, purporting that Lord Turbisha, to amuse the ladies, would fight with any captain among the Austrian troops. Smith accepted the challenge.

Flags of truce were exchanged between the two armies, and crowds of fair dames and fearless men assembled to witness the combat. Lord Turbisha entered the field well mounted and armed.

On his shoulders were fixed two large wings made of eagles' feathers, set in silver, and richly ornamented with gold and precious stones. A janizary, or Turkish soldier, bore his lance before him, and another followed, leading a horse superbly caparisoned.

Smith came upon the ground with less parade. A flourish of trumpets preceded him, and his lance was supported by a single page.

The Turk fell at the first charge, and Smith returned to his army in triumph. This so enraged one of the friends of the slain that he sent a challenge to Smith, offering him his head, his horse, and his armor, if he dared come and take them.

The challenge was accepted, and the combatants came upon the ground with nearly the same ceremony and splendor. Their lances broke at the first charge, without doing injury to either; but, at the second onset, the Turk was wounded, thrown from his horse, and killed.

The Christian army, anxious to finish erecting some fortifications, was very willing to amuse their enemies in this way. They therefore persuaded Captain Smith to send a challenge in his turn, offering his head, in payment for the two he had won to any one who had skill and strength enough to take it.

The offer was accepted; a third Turk tried his fortune with the bold adventurer. This time Captain Smith was nearly unhorsed; however, by his dexterity and judgment, he recovered himself and soon returned to the camp victorious.

These warlike deeds met with much applause. And the prince gave him a coat of arms, signed with the royal seal, representing three Turk's heads on a white field.

Not long after this, Captain Smith was left wounded on the field of battle, was taken prisoner by the Turks, and sent as a slave to a noble lady in the interior of the country.

He could speak Italian well, and his fair mistress was very fond of that language. She listened to accounts of his bravery, his adventures, and his misfortunes with deepening interest; she finally sent him to her brother, with a request that he should be treated with much kindness.

The proud officer was angry that his sister should trouble herself about a vile European slave; and, instead of attending to her request, he caused him to be loaded with irons and abused in the most shameful manner.

During the long and tedious period of his slavery, he suffered as much as it is possible for man to endure; but at length he killed his tyrannical master and, with great peril, escaped through the deserts into Russia.

His romantic genius would not long allow him to remain easy. He could not be happy unless he was engaged in daring and adventurous actions. He no sooner heard of an expedition to Virginia, under the command of Christopher Newport, than he resolved to join it.

He arrived in this country with the first emigrants, who settled in Jamestown, April 26, 1607. It is said this infant settlement must have perished had it not been for the courage and ingenuity of Captain Smith.

Once they were all nearly dying with hunger, and the savages utterly refused to sell them any food. In this extremity, Smith stole the Indian idol, Okee, which was made of skins stuffed with moss and would not return it until the Indians sold them as much corn as they wanted.

The colony was once in imminent danger of losing their brave and intelligent friend. While exploring the source of the Chickahominy river, he imprudently left his companions and, while alone, was seen and pursued by a party of savages. He retreated fighting, killed three Indians with his own hand, and probably would have regained his boat in safety, had he not accidentally plunged into a miry hole from which he could not extricate himself.

By this accident, he was taken prisoner. The Indians would have tortured him and put him to death, according to their cruel customs, had not his ever-ready wit come to his aid.

He showed them a small ivory compass, which he had with him and, by signs, explained many wonderful things to them. His enemies were inspired with a most profound respect and resolved not to kill the extraordinary man without consulting their chief.

He was brought into the presence of King Powhatan. The Indian Chief, dressed in a robe of raccoon skins, was seated on a kind of throne with two beautiful young daughters at his side. After a long consultation, he was condemned to die.

Two large stones were brought. His head was laid upon one of them, and the war clubs were raised to strike the deadly blow. At this moment, Pocahontas, the king's favorite daughter, sprang forward, threw herself between him and the executioners, and by her entreaties saved his life.

Powhatan promised him that he should return to Jamestown, if the English would give him a certain quantity of ammunition and trinkets. Smith agreed to obtain them, provided a messenger would carry a leaf to his companions. On this leaf he briefly stated what must be sent.

Powhatan had never heard of writing; he laughed at the idea that a leaf could speak and regarded the whole as an imposition on the part of the prisoner.

When, however, the messenger returned with the promised ransom, he regarded Smith as nothing less than a wizard and gladly allowed him to depart. It seemed to be the fate of this singular man to excite a powerful interest wherever he went.

Pocahontas had such a deep attachment for him that, in 1609 when only fourteen years old, she stole away from her tribe and, during a most dreary night, walked to Jamestown to tell him that her father had formed the design of cutting off the whole English settlement. Thus, at the hazard of her own, she saved his life a second time.

This charming Indian girl did not meet with all the gratitude she deserved. After the departure of Captain Smith, who had returned to England for surgical aid necessitated by a wound, a copper kettle was offered to any Indian who would bring Pocahontas to the English settlement. She was, accordingly, stolen from her father and carried prisoner to Jamestown. Powhatan offered five hundred bushels of corn as a ransom for his darling child.

Before the negotiation was finished, an Englishman of good character, by the name of Thomas Rolfe, became attached to Pocahontas, and they were soon after married with the king's consent. This event secured peace to the English for many years.

The Indian bride became a Christian and was baptized. In 1616, Pocahontas went to England with her husband, was introduced at court, and received great attention. Pocahontas never returned to her native country. She died at Gravesend in 1617 just as she was about to embark for America. She left one son, Thomas Rolfe; from whose daughter were descended several people of high rank in Virginia, among whom was the celebrated John Randolph of Roanoke.

Smith had many adventures after his wound obliged him to leave Jamestown. He visited this country again, made a voyage to the Summer Isles, fought with pirates, joined the French against the Spaniards, and was adrift, in a little boat, alone, on the stormy sea, during a night so tempestuous that thirteen French ships were wrecked, near the Isle of Re. Yet he alone was saved.

He died in London, in 1631, in the fifty-second year of his age, after having published his singular adventures in Europe, Asia, Africa, and America.

Written Summation

Two large stones were brought. His head was laid upon one of them, and the war clubs were raised to strike the deadly blow. At this moment, Pocahontas, the king's favorite daughter, sprang forward, threw herself between him and the executioners, and by her entreaties saved his life.

Model Pracitce 1

Model Practice 2

Model Practice 3

A White Boy among the Indians
by Edward Eggleston

Among the people that came to Virginia in 1609, two years after the colony was planted, was a boy named Henry Spelman. He was the son of a well-known man. He had been a bad and troublesome boy in England, and his family sent him to Virginia, thinking that he might be better in the new country. At least his friends thought he would not trouble them so much when he was so far away.

Many hundreds of people came at the same time that Henry Spelman did. Captain John Smith was then governor of the little colony. He was puzzled to know how to feed all these people; as many of them were troublesome, he was still more puzzled to know how to govern them.

In order not to have so many to feed, he sent some of them to live among the Indians here and there. A chief called Little Powhatan asked Smith to send some of his men to live with him. The Indians wanted the white men to live among them, so they could learn to make the things that the white men had. Captain Smith agreed to give the boy Henry Spelman to Little Powhatan in exchange for a place to plant a new settlement.

Spelman stayed awhile with the chief, and then he went back to the English at Jamestown.

But when he came to Jamestown he was sorry that he had not stayed among the Indians. Captain John Smith had gone home to England. George Percy was now governor of the English. They had very little food to eat, and Spelman began to be afraid that he might starve to death with the rest of them. Powhatan, who was chief over all the other chiefs in the area, sent a white man who was living with him to carry some deer meat to Jamestown. When it came time for this white man to go back, he asked that some of his countrymen might go to the Indian country with him. The governor sent Spelman, who was glad enough to go to the Indians again because they had plenty of food to eat.

Three weeks after this, Powhatan sent Henry Spelman back to Jamestown to tell the English that if they would come to his country and bring him some copper he would give them some corn for it. The Indians at this time had no iron, and what little copper they had they bought from other Indians who probably got it from the copper mines far away on Lake Superior.

The English greatly needed corn; so they took a boat and went up to the Indian country with copper, in order to buy corn. They quarreled with the Indians about the measurement of the corn. The Indians hid themselves near the water, and while the white men were carrying the corn on their vessel, the Indians killed some of them. About this time, seeing that the white men were so hungry, the Indians began to hope that they would be able to drive them all out of the country.

Spelman and a Dutchman, who also lived with Powhatan, began to be afraid that he would not protect them any longer. So, when a chief of the Potomac Indians visited Powhatan and asked the Dutchman and the boy to go to his country, they left Powhatan and went back with them. Powhatan sent his Indians after them. They killed the Dutchman, but Henry Spelman ran away into the woods. Powhatan's men followed him, but the Potomacs reached Powhatan's men and held them back until Spelman could get away. The boy managed at last to get to the country of the Potomac Indians.

It was very lucky for Spelman that he was among the Indians at this time. Nearly all the white people in Jamestown were killed or died of hunger. Spelman lived among the Indians for years and acted as a translator between the English and the Indians.

Written Summation

Powhatan sent his Indians after them. They killed the Dutchman, but Henry Spelman ran away into the woods. Powhatan's men followed him, but the Potomacs reached Powhatan's men and held them back until Spelman could get away. The boy managed at last to get to the country of the Potomac Indians.

Model Practice 1

Model Practice 2

Model Practice 3

The Pine-Tree Shillings
by Nathaniel Hawthorne

Captain John Hull was the mint-master of Massachusetts and coined all the money that was made there. This was a new line of business, for in the earlier days of the colony, the current coinage consisted of gold and silver money of England, Portugal, and Spain.

These coins being scarce, the people were often forced to barter their commodities, instead of selling them. For instance, if a man wanted to buy a coat, he, perhaps, exchanged a bearskin for it. If he wished for a barrel of molasses, he might purchase it with a pile of pine-boards. Musket-bullets were used instead of farthings.

The Indians had a sort of money, called wampum, which was made of clamshells; and this strange sort of specie was, likewise, taken in payment of debts by the English settlers. Bank bills had never been heard of. There was not money enough of any kind, in many parts of the country, to pay the salaries of the ministers; so they sometimes had to take quintals of fish, bushels of corn, or cords of wood, instead of silver or gold.

As the people grew more numerous, and their trade one with another increased, the want of current money was still more sensibly felt. To supply the demand, the general court passed a law for establishing a coinage of shillings, sixpences, and threepences. Captain John Hull was appointed to manufacture this money and was to have one shilling, out of every twenty, to pay him for the trouble of making them.

Hereupon, all the old silver in the colony was handed over to Captain John Hull. The battered cans, tankards, buckles, broken spoons, silver-buttons of worn-out coats, and silver hilts of swords that had figured at courts, all such curious old articles were, doubtless, thrown into the melting pot together. But by far the greater part of the silver consisted of bullion from the mines of South America, which the English buccaneers, who were little better than pirates, had taken from the Spaniards and brought to Massachusetts.

All this old and new silver being melted down and coined, the result was an immense amount of splendid shillings, sixpences, and threepences. Each had the date, 1652, on the one side and the figure of a pine-tree on the other. Hence, they were called pine-tree shillings. And for every twenty shillings that he coined, you will remember, Captain John Hull was entitled to put one shilling into his own pocket.

The magistrates soon began to suspect that the mint-master would have the best of the bargain. They offered him a large sum of money, if he would give up that twentieth shilling, which he was continually dropping into his own pocket. But Captain Hull declared himself perfectly satisfied with the shilling. And well he might be; for so diligently did he labor that in a few years his pockets, his money-bags, and his strong box were overflowing with pine-tree shillings.

When the mint-master had grown very rich, a young man, Samuel Sewell by name, fell in love with his only daughter. His daughter, whom we will call Betsey, was a fine, hearty damsel, by no means so slender as some young ladies of our own days. As Samuel was a young man of good character, industrious in his business, and a member of the church, the mint-master very readily gave his consent.

"Yes; you may take her," said he, in his rough way; "and you'll find her a heavy burden enough!" On the wedding-day, we may suppose that honest John Hull dressed himself in a plum-colored coat, all the buttons of which were made of pine-tree shillings. The buttons of his waistcoat were sixpences, and the knees of his smallclothes were buttoned with silver threepences.

There, too, was the bridegroom, dressed in a fine purple coat and gold-lace waistcoat, with as much other finery as the Puritan laws and customs would allow him to put on. His hair was cropped close to his head, because Governor Endicott had forbidden any man to wear it below the ears. But he was a very personable young man; so thought the bridesmaids and Miss Betsey herself.

The mint-master was pleased with his new son-in-law; especially since he had courted Miss Betsey, out of pure love, and had said nothing at all about her portion. So, when the marriage ceremony was over, Captain Hull whispered to two of his men-servants who immediately went out and soon returned lugging in a large pair of scales. They were such a pair as wholesale merchants use for weighing bulky commodities, and quite a bulky commodity was now to be weighed in them.

"Daughter Betsey," said the mint-master, "get into one side of these scales." Miss Betsey, or Mrs. Sewell, as we must now call her, did as she was bid, like a dutiful child, without any question of the why and wherefore. But what her father could mean, unless to make her husband pay for her by the pound, in which case she would have been a dear bargain, she had not the least idea.

"And now," said honest John Hull to the servants, "bring that box hither." The box, to which the mint-master pointed, was a huge, square, ironbound, oaken chest. The servants tugged with might and main, but they could not lift this enormous receptacle and were finally obliged to drag it across the floor.

Captain Hull then took a key from his girdle, unlocked the chest, and lifted its ponderous lid. Behold! It was full to the brim of bright pine-tree shillings, fresh from the mint; Samuel Sewell began to think that his father-in-law had gotten possession of all the money in the Massachusetts' treasury. But it was only the mint-master's honest share of the coinage.

Then the servants, at Captain Hull's command, heaped double handfuls of shillings into one side of the scales while Betsey remained in the other. Jingle, jingle went the shillings as handful after handful was thrown in until, plump and ponderous as she was, they fairly weighed the young lady from the floor.

"There, son Samuel," said the honest mint-master, resuming his seat, "take these shillings for my daughter's portion. Use her kindly, and thank Heaven for her. It is not every wife that's worth her weight in silver!"

Written Summation

Captain Hull then took a key from his girdle, unlocked the chest, and lifted its ponderous lid. Behold! It was full to the brim of bright pine-tree shillings, fresh from the mint; Samuel Sewell began to think that his father-in-law had gotten possession of all the money in the Massachusetts' treasury. But it was only the mint-master's honest share of the coinage.

Model Practice 1

Model Practice 2

Model Practice 3

Sir Isaac Newton
by Nathaniel Hawthorne

On Christmas day in the year 1642, Isaac Newton was born at the small village of Woolsthorpe, in England. Little did his mother think when she beheld her newborn babe, that he was destined to explain many matters which had been a mystery ever since the creation of the world.

Isaac's father being dead, Mrs. Newton was married again to a clergyman, and went to reside at North Witham. Her son was left to the care of his good old grandmother, who was very kind to him and sent him to school. In his early years Isaac did not appear to be a very bright scholar, but was chiefly remarkable for his ingenuity in all mechanical occupations. He had a set of little tools and saws of various sizes manufactured by himself. With the aid of these Isaac contrived to make many curious articles, at which he worked with so much skill that he seemed to have been born with a saw or chisel in hand.

Not far from his grandmother's residence there was a windmill which operated on a new plan. Isaac was in the habit of going thither frequently and would spend whole hours in examining its various parts.

While the mill was at rest, he pried into its internal machinery. When its broad sails were set in motion by the wind, he watched the process by which the millstones were made to revolve and crush the grain that was put into the hopper. After gaining a thorough knowledge of its construction, he was observed to be unusually busy with his tools.

It was not long before his grandmother and all the neighborhood knew what Isaac had been about. He had constructed a model of the windmill. Though not so large, I suppose, as one of the box traps, which boys set to catch squirrels, yet every part of the mill and its machinery was complete. Its little sails were neatly made of linen and whirled round very swiftly when the mill was placed in a draught of air. Even a puff of wind from Isaac's mouth or from a pair of bellows was sufficient to set the sails in motion. And, what was most curious, if a handful of grains of wheat were put into the little hopper, they would soon be converted into snow-white flour.

Isaac's playmates were enchanted with his new windmill. They thought that nothing so pretty and so wonderful had ever been seen in the whole world.

"But, Isaac," said one of them, "you have forgotten one thing that belongs to a mill."

"What is that?" asked Isaac, for he supposed that, from the roof of the mill to its foundation, he had forgotten nothing.

"Why, where is the miller?" said his friend.

"That is true, I must look out for one," said Isaac; so he set himself to consider how the deficiency should be supplied.

He might easily have made the miniature figure of a man; but then it would not have been able to move about and perform the duties of a miller. As Captain Lemuel Gulliver had not yet discovered the island of Lilliput, Isaac did not know that there were little men in the world whose size was just suited to his windmill. It so happened, however, that a mouse had just been caught in the trap, and as no other miller could be found, Mr. Mouse was appointed to that important office. The new miller made a very respectable appearance in his dark gray coat. To be sure, he had not a very good character for honesty and was suspected of sometimes stealing a portion of the grain, which was given him to grind. But perhaps some two-legged millers are quite as dishonest as this small quadruped.

Written Summation

It was not long before his grandmother and all the neighborhood knew what Isaac had been about. He had constructed a model of the windmill. Though not so large, I suppose, as one of the box traps, which boys set to catch squirrels, yet every part of the mill and its machinery was complete. Its little sails were neatly made of linen and whirled round very swiftly when the mill was placed in a draught of air.

Model Practice 1

Model Practice 2

Model Practice 3

King Philip to the White Settler
by Edward Everett

Think of the country for which the Indians fought. Who can blame them? As Philip looked down from his seat on Mount Hope, that glorious eminence, that

"----throne of royal state, which far
Outshone the wealth of Ormus and of Ind,
Or where the gorgeous East, with richest hand,
Showers on her kings barbaric pearl and gold,"--

as he looked down, and beheld the lovely scene which spread beneath at a summer sunset, the distant hill-tops glittering as with fire, the slanting beams streaming across the waters, the broad plains, the island groups, the majestic forest—could he be blamed if his heart burned within him as he beheld it all passing, by no tardy process, from beneath his control into the hands of the stranger?

As the river chieftains —the lords of the waterfalls and the mountains —ranged this lovely valley, can it be wondered at, if they beheld with bitterness the forest disappearing beneath the settler's ax, the fishing-place disturbed by his saw-mills? Can we not fancy the feelings with which some strong-minded savage, the chief of the Pocomtuck Indians who should have ascended the summit of the Sugar-loaf Mountain (rising as it does before us, at this moment, in all its loveliness and grandeur) in company with a friendly settler, contemplating the progress already made by the white man and marking the gigantic strides with which he was advancing into the wilderness, should fold his arms and say, "White man, there is eternal war between me and thee! I quit not the land of my fathers but with my life. In those woods, where I bent my youthful bow, I will still hunt the deer; over yonder waters I will still glide, unrestrained, in my bark canoe. By those dashing waterfalls I will still lay up my winter's store of food; on these fertile meadows I will still plant my corn.

"Stranger, the land is mine! I understand not these paper rights. I gave not my consent when, as thou sayest, these broad regions were purchased, for a few baubles, of my fathers. They could sell what was theirs; they could sell no more. How could my fathers sell that which the Great Spirit sent me into the world to live upon? They knew not what they did.

"The stranger came, a timid suppliant, few and feeble, and asked to lie down on the red man's bearskin, and warm himself at the red man's fire, and have a little piece of land to raise corn for his women and children; and now he is become strong, and mighty, and bold, and spreads out his parchments over the whole, and says, 'It is mine.'

"Stranger! There is not room for us both. The Great Spirit has not made us to live together. There is poison in the white man's cup; the white man's dog barks at the red man's heels. If I should leave the land of my fathers, whither shall I fly? Shall I go to the south and dwell among the graves of the Pequots? Shall I wander to the west, the fierce Mohawk, the man-eater, is my foe. Shall I fly to the east, the great water is before me. No, stranger, here I have lived, and here will I die. And if here thou abidest, there is eternal war between me and thee.

"Thou hast taught me thy arts of destruction; for that alone I thank thee. And now take heed to thy steps; the red man is thy foe. When thou goest forth by day, my bullet shall whistle past thee; when thou liest down by night, my knife is at thy throat. The noonday sun shall not discover thy enemy, and the darkness of midnight shall not protect thy rest. Thou shalt plant in terror, and I will reap in blood; thou shalt sow the earth with corn, and I will strew it with ashes; thou shalt go forth with the sickle, and I will follow after with the scalping-knife; thou shalt build, and I will burn—till the white man or the Indian perish from the land. Go thy way for this time in safety, but remember, stranger, there is eternal war between me and thee!"

Written Summation

Stranger, the land is mine! I understand not these paper rights. I gave not my consent when, as thou sayest, these broad regions were purchased, for a few baubles, of my fathers. They could sell what was theirs; they could sell no more. How could my fathers sell that which the Great Spirit sent me into the world to live upon? They knew not what they did.

Model Practice 1

Model Practice 2

Model Practice 3

King Charles II and William Penn
by Mason L. Weems

King Charles: Well, friend William! I have sold you a noble province in North America; but still, I suppose you have no thoughts of going thither yourself?

Penn: Yes, I have, I assure thee, friend Charles; and I am just come to bid thee farewell.

King Charles: What! Venture yourself among the savages of North America! Why, man, what security have you that you will not be in their war kettle in two hours after setting foot on their shores?

Penn: The best security in the world.

King Charles: I doubt that, friend William; I have no idea of any security against those cannibals but in a regiment of good soldiers, with their muskets and bayonets. And mind, I tell you beforehand, that, with all my good will for you and your family, to whom I am under obligations, I will not send a single soldier with you.

Penn: I want none of thy soldiers, Charles: I depend on something better than thy soldiers.

King Charles: Ah! What may that be?

Penn: Why, I depend upon themselves; on the working of their own hearts; on their notions of justice; on their moral sense.

King Charles: A fine thing, this same moral sense, no doubt; but I fear you will not find much of it among the Indians of North America.

Penn: And why not among them as well as others?

King Charles: Because if they had possessed any, they would not have treated my subjects so barbarously as they have done.

Penn: That is no proof of the contrary, friend Charles. Thy subjects were the aggressors. When thy subjects first went to North America, they found these poor people the fondest and kindest creatures in the world. Every day they would watch for them to come ashore, and hasten to meet them, and feast them on the best fish, and venison, and corn, which were all they had. In return for this hospitality of the savages, as we call them, thy subjects, termed Christians, seized on their country and rich hunting grounds for farms for themselves. Now, is it to be wondered at, that these much-injured people should have been driven to desperation by such injustice; and that, burning with revenge, they should have committed some excesses?

King Charles: Well, then, I hope you will not complain when they come to treat you in the same manner.

Penn: I am not afraid of it.

King Charles: Ah! How will you avoid it? You mean to get their hunting grounds, too, I suppose?

Penn: Yes, but not by driving these poor people away from them.

King Charles: No, indeed? How then will you get their lands?

Penn: I mean to buy their lands of them.

King Charles: Buy their lands of them? Why, man, you have already bought them of me!

Penn: Yes, I know I have, and at a dear rate, too; but I did it only to get thy good will, not that I thought thou hadst any right to their lands.

King Charles: How, man? No right to their lands?

Penn: No, friend Charles, no right; no right at all: what right hast thou to their lands?

King Charles: Why, the right of discovery, to be sure; the right which the Pope and all Christian kings have agreed to give one another.

Penn: The right of discovery? A strange kind of right, indeed. Now suppose, friend Charles, that some canoe load of these Indians, crossing the sea and discovering this island of Great Britain, were to claim it as their own and set it up for sale over thy head, what wouldst thou think of it?

King Charles: Why—why—why—I must confess, I should think it a piece of great impudence in them.

Penn: Well, then, how canst thou, a Christian, and a Christian prince, too, do that which thou so utterly condemnest in these people whom thou callest savages? And suppose, again, that these Indians, on thy refusal to give up thy island of Great Britain, were to make war on thee, and having weapons more destructive than thine, were to destroy many of thy subjects and drive the rest away—wouldst thou not think it horribly cruel?

King Charles: I must say, friend William, that I should; how can I say otherwise?

Penn: Well, then, how can I, who call myself a Christian, do what I should abhor even in the heathen? No. I will not do it. But I will buy the right of the proper owners, even of the Indians themselves. By doing this, I shall imitate God himself in his justice and mercy, and thereby, insure his blessing on my colony, if I should ever live to plant one in North America.

Written Summation

Well, then how can I, who call myself a Christian, do what I should abhor even in the heathen? No. I will not do it. But I will buy the right of the proper owners, even of the Indians themselves. By doing this, I shall imitate God himself in his justice and mercy and thereby insure his blessing on my colony, if I should ever live to plant one in North America.

Model Practice 1

Model Practice 2

Model Practice 3

The Whistle
by Benjamin Franklin

When I was a boy of seven years old, my friends, on a holiday, filled my pocket with coppers. I went directly to a shop where they sold toys for children, and being charmed with the sound of a whistle, that I met by the way in the hands of another boy, I voluntarily offered and gave all my money for one. I then came home and went whistling all over the house, much pleased with my whistle but disturbing all the family. My brothers, and sisters, and cousins, understanding the bargain I had made, told me I had given four times as much for it as it was worth. Put me in mind what good things I might have bought with the rest of the money; and laughed at me so much for my folly, that I cried with vexation. And the reflection gave me more chagrin than the whistle gave me pleasure.

This, however, was afterwards of use to me, the impression continuing in my mind; so that often, when I was tempted to buy some unnecessary thing, I said to myself: "Don't give too much for the whistle;" and I saved my money.

As I grew up, came into the world, and observed the actions of men, I thought I met with many, very many, who gave too much for the whistle.

When I saw any one fond of popularity, constantly employing himself in politics, neglecting his own affairs and ruining them by that neglect, "He pays, indeed," said I, "too much for his whistle."

If I saw one fond of fine clothes, fine furniture, fine horses, all above his fortune, for which he contracted debts and ended his career in poverty, "Alas!" said I, "he has paid dear, very dear, for his whistle."

In short, I believed that a great part of the miseries of mankind were brought upon them by the false estimates they had made of the value of things, and by their giving too much for their whistles.

Written Summation

If I saw one fond of fine clothes, fine furniture, fine horses, all above his fortune, for which he contracted debts and ended his career in poverty, "Alas!" said I, "he has paid dear, very dear, for his whistle."

In short, I believed that a great part of the miseries of mankind were brought upon them by the false estimates they had made of the value of things, and by their giving too much for their whistles.

Model Practice 1

Model Practice 2

Model Practice 3

Young Benjamin Franklin
by Nathaniel Hawthorne

When Benjamin Franklin was a boy, he was very fond of fishing; and many of his leisure hours were spent on the margin of the millpond catching flounders, perch, and eels that came up thither with the tide.

The place where Ben and his playmates did most of their fishing was a marshy spot on the outskirts of Boston. On the edge of the water, there was a deep bed of clay, in which the boys were forced to stand while they caught their fish.

"This is very uncomfortable," said Ben Franklin one day to his comrades, while they were standing in the quagmire.

"So it is," said the other boys. "What a pity we have no better place to stand on!"

On the dry land, not far from the quagmire, there were at that time a great many large stones that had been brought there to be used in building the foundation of a new house. Ben mounted upon the highest of these stones.

"Boys," said he, "I have thought of a plan. You know what a plague it is to have to stand in the quagmire yonder. See I am bedaubed to the knees, and you are all in the same plight.

"Now I propose that we build a wharf. You see these stones? The workmen mean to use them for building a house here. My plan is to take these same stones, carry them to the edge of the water, and build a wharf with them. What say you, lads? Shall we build the wharf?"

"Yes, yes," cried the boys; "let's set about it!"

It was agreed that they should all be on the spot that evening, and begin their grand public enterprise by moonlight.

Accordingly, at the appointed time, the boys met and eagerly began to remove the stones. They worked like a colony of ants, sometimes two or three of them taking hold of one stone; and at last they had carried them all away, and built their little wharf.

"Now, boys," cried Ben, when the job was done, "let's give three cheers, and go home to bed. To-morrow we may catch fish at our ease."

"Hurrah! Hurrah! Hurrah!" shouted his comrades, and all scampered off home and to bed, to dream of to-morrow's sport.

In the morning, the masons came to begin their work. But what was their surprise to find the stones all gone! The master mason, looking carefully on the ground, saw the tracks of many little feet, some with shoes and some barefoot. Following these to the waterside, he soon found what had become of the missing building stones.

"Ah! I see what the mischief is," said he; "those little rascals who were here yesterday have stolen the stones to build a wharf with. And I must say that they understand their business well."

He was so angry that he at once went to make a complaint before the magistrate; and his Honor wrote an order to "take the bodies of Benjamin Franklin, and other evil-disposed persons," who had stolen a heap of stones.

If the owner of the stolen property had not been more merciful than the master mason, it might have gone hard with our friend Benjamin and his comrades. But, luckily for them, the gentleman had a respect for Ben's father, and moreover, was pleased with the spirit of the whole affair. He therefore let the culprits off easily.

But the poor boys had to go through another trial, and receive sentence, and suffer punishment, too, from their own fathers. Many a rod was worn to the stump on that unlucky night. As for Ben, he was less afraid of a whipping than of his father's reproof. And, indeed, his father was very much disturbed.

"Benjamin, come hither," began Mr. Franklin in his usual stern and weighty tone. The boy approached and stood before his father's chair. "Benjamin," said his father, "what could induce you to take property which did not belong to you?"

"Why, father," replied Ben, hanging his head at first, but then lifting his eyes to Mr. Franklin's face, "if it had been merely for my own benefit, I never should have dreamed of it. But I knew that the wharf would be a public convenience. If the owner of the stones should build a house with them, nobody would enjoy any advantage but himself. Now, I made use of them in a way that was for the advantage of many persons."

"My son," said Mr. Franklin solemnly, "so far as it was in your power, you have done a greater harm to the public than to the owner of the stones. I do verily believe, Benjamin, that almost all the public and private misery of mankind arises from a neglect of this great truth—that evil can produce only evil, that good ends must be wrought out by good means."

To the end of his life, Ben Franklin never forgot this conversation with his father; and we have reason to suppose that, in most of his public and private career, he sought to act upon the principles which that good and wise man then taught him.

Written Summation

"My son," said Mr. Franklin solemnly, "so far as it was in your power, you have done a greater harm to the public than to the owner of the stones. I do verily believe, Benjamin, that almost all the public and private misery of mankind arises from a neglect of this great truth—that evil can produce only evil, that good ends must be wrought out by good means."

Model Practice 1

Model Practice 2

Model Practice 3

Little Lord Sold into Bondage
by Edward Eggleston

There lived in Ireland, a long time ago, a certain Lord Altham. The time was about sixty years before our American Revolution. This Lord Altham was a weak and foolish man. He quarreled with his wife and sent her away. He wasted his money in wicked living and got into debt. He had a little son named James Annesley. Jemmy, as he was called, was sent to a boarding school; but the father grew more wicked and careless of his son. He sent the boy away and pretended that he was dead. He did this because he wanted to sell some property that he could not sell if Jemmy were alive.

Jemmy found himself badly treated where he lived. When he complained, he was told that his father did not pay his board; so he ran away. He lived in the streets with rough boys. He ran errands for pay, like the other little street boys. But still the boys knew that Jemmy was the son of a lord. Strangers were surprised to hear a little ragged boy called "my lord" by his playmates.

When he was about thirteen years old, his father died. Then Jemmy Annesley became Lord Altham in place of his father; but his Uncle Richard, who was a cruel man, took Jemmy's property and called himself Lord Altham.

The wicked uncle was afraid that people would find out that Jemmy was alive, so he sent a man to see where the boy was. When the boy was found, his uncle accused him of stealing a silver spoon. He hired three policemen to arrest the boy and put him on a ship. Poor Jemmy wept bitterly. He told the people he was afraid his uncle would kill him. The ship took him to Philadelphia, where he was sold to a farmer to serve until he should be of age.

One day when he was about seventeen years old, he came into his master's house with a gun in one hand and a squirrel in the other. There were two strangers sitting by the fire. They had found the door open and had walked in.

One of the men said, "Are you a servant in this house?"

"I am," said James.

"What country did you come from?"

"Ireland."

"We are from Ireland ourselves," said one of the strange men. "What part of Ireland are you from?"

"From the county of Wexford."

"We are from that county. What is your name?"

"James Annesley."

"I never heard that name there," said the traveler.

"Did you know Lord Altham?" asked the boy.

"Yes."

"Well, I am his son."

"What!" cried the stranger, "you the son of Lord Altham! Impossible!"

But the young man insisted that he was Lord Altham's son.

"Tell me how Lord Altham's house stands," said the stranger.

The young man told him enough to prove that he knew all about the place. The stranger said that if James ever came to Ireland to claim his estate, he would do what he could to help him.

James Annesley was badly treated by his master. At length he ran away, but he was retaken and was put into a jail in Lancaster. He was kept in prison a good while. He had a fine voice, and he amused himself by singing. The people used to stand outside of the jail to hear him sing.

For running away he was obliged to serve a still longer time. He spent thirteen years in slavery.

When he got free at last, he told Mr. Ellis of Philadelphia about his case. This kind-hearted man gave him a passage on a ship going to the West Indies. An English fleet was then in the West Indies. It was commanded by the famous Admiral Vernon. When the brave admiral heard James Annesley's story, he took him to England. In England James found friends ready to help him.

There was a long lawsuit, but James's old friends and schoolmates came to court as witnesses for him. One of the men who had talked with him while he was a servant in Pennsylvania told the Court about it. Two of the policemen that had helped to put little Jemmy on shipboard confessed the dreadful act they had done.

Then the jury gave a verdict that James Annesley was the true Lord Altham. There was great joy among the people, and everybody detested the cruel uncle. The people made songs about him and sang them under his windows. James Annesley was now called Lord Altham. But before the young lord came into possession of his title and his property, he was taken ill and died.

Written Summation

The wicked uncle was afraid that people would find out that Jemmy was alive, so he sent a man to see where the boy was. When the boy was found, his uncle accused him of stealing a silver spoon. He hired three policemen to arrest the boy and put him on a ship. Poor Jemmy wept bitterly.

Model Practice 1

Model Practice 2

Model Practice 3

The Story of Peter Williamson—Twice a Slave
by Edward Eggleston

One day a boy named Peter Williamson was walking along the streets of Aberdeen in Scotland. The little fellow was eight years old. Two men met him and asked him to go on board a ship with them. When he got on board, he was put down in the lower part of the ship with other boys. The ship sailed to America with twenty boys who, like Peter, had been stolen from their parents. They were taken to Philadelphia and sold to work for seven years.

Little Peter was lucky enough to fall into the hands of a kind master. Among those who came to buy boys off this ship was a man who had himself been stolen from Scotland when he was young. He felt sorry for little Peter when he saw him put up for sale. The price the cruel captain asked for him was about fifty dollars. The Scotchman paid this money and took Peter for his boy. He sent him to school in the winter and treated him kindly. Peter, for his part, was a good boy and did his work faithfully. He stayed with his master after his time was finished.

When Peter was about seventeen years old, this good master died. He left to Peter about six hundred dollars in money for being a good boy. He also gave him his best horse and saddle and all his own clothes. Some years after this, Peter married and went to live in the northern part of Pennsylvania. He was by this time a man of property.

One night, when his wife was away from home, the Indians came to his house. He got a gun and ran upstairs. He pointed the gun at the Indians, but they told him that if he did not shoot they would not kill him. So he came down and gave himself up as a prisoner.

The Indians treated him very cruelly. He was with them more than a year. His sufferings were so great that he wished sometimes that he were dead. He knew that if he ran away the Indians would probably catch him and kill him in some cruel way. But one night, when the Indians were all asleep, he resolved to take the risk. You may believe that when he had started he ran with all his might.

When daylight came, he hid himself in a hollow tree. After a while, he heard the Indians running all about the tree. He could hear them tell one another how they would kill him when they found him. But they did not think to look into the tree.

The next night he ran on again. He came very near running into a camp of Indians. But at last he came in sight of a friend's house. He was tired, starving, and had hardly any clothes left on him. He knocked at the door. The woman who saw him thought that he was an Indian. She screamed, and the man of the house got his gun to kill him. But he quickly told his friend that he was no Indian, but Peter Williamson. Everybody had given him up for dead, but now all his friends were happy to see him alive. He had twice been carried into slavery, once by cruel white men and once by cruel red men.

Written Summation

One night, when his wife was away from home, the Indians came to his house. He got a gun and ran upstairs. He pointed the gun at the Indians, but they told him that if he did not shoot they would not kill him. So he came down and gave himself up as a prisoner.

Model Practice 1

Model Practice 2

Model Practice 3

The Intrepid Youth
by Charles W. Sanders

It was a calm, sunny day in the year 1750, the scene—a piece of forestland in the north of Virginia, near a noble stream of water. Implements of surveying were lying about, and several men reclining under the trees, betokened, by their dress and appearance, that they composed a party engaged in laying out the wild lands of the country.

These persons had apparently just finished their dinner. Apart from the group, walked a young man of a tall and compact frame who moved with the elastic tread of one accustomed to contant exercise in the open air. His countenance wore a look of decision and manliness not usually found in one so young, for he was apparently little over eighteen years of age. His hat had been cast off, as if for comfort, and he had paused, with one foot advanced, in a graceful and natural attitude.

Suddenly there was a shriek, then another, and several in rapid succession. The voice was that of a woman and seemed to proceed from the other side of a dense thicket. At the first scream the youth turned his head in the direction of the sound. But when it was repeated he pushed aside the undergrowth that separated him from it, and quickening his footsteps as the cries succeeded each other in alarming rapidity, he soon dashed into an open space on the banks of the stream where stood a rude log cabin.

As the young man broke from the undergrowth, he saw his companions crowded together on the banks of the river, while in the midst stood the shrieking woman, who was being held back by two of the men but was struggling vigorously for freedom. It was but the work of a moment for the young man to make his way through the crowd and confront the female.

The instant her eye fell on him, she exclaimed, "Oh! Sir, you will do something for me. Make them release me—for the love of God! My boy—my poor boy is drowning, and they will not let me go!"

"It would be madness; she will jump into the river," said one of the men, "and the rapids would dash her to pieces in a moment!"

Several of the men approached the brink and were on the point of springing in after the child when the sight of the sharp rocks crowding the channel, the rush and whirl of the waters, and the want of any knowledge where to look for the boy deterred them. And they gave up the enterprise, not so with the noble youth.

He threw off his coat and sprung to the edge of the bank. Here he stood for a moment, running his eyes rapidly over the scene below, determining with a glance the different currents and the most dangerous of the rocks, in order to shape his course when in the stream. He had scarcely formed his conclusion when he saw in the water a white object, which he knew to be the boy's dress, and he plunged into the wild and roaring rapids.

"Thank God, he will save my child," cried the mother; "There he is!—Oh! My boy, my darling boy, how could I leave you!"

Every one had rushed to the brink of the precipice and was now following with eager eyes the progress of the youth, as the current bore him onward, like a feather in the embrace of the hurricane. Now it seemed as if he would be dashed against a jutting rock, over which the water flew in foam, and a whirlpool would drag him in, from whose grasp escape would appear impossible.

At times, the current bore him under, and he would be lost to sight; then, just as the spectators gave him up, he would appear though far from where he vanished, still buffeting amid the vortex. Oh, how that mother's straining eyes followed him in his perilous career. How her heart sunk when he went under. And what a gush of joy she felt when she saw him emerging again from the waters, flinging the waves aside with his athletic arms, and struggling on in pursuit of her boy!

But it seemed as if his generous efforts were not to avail; for though the current was bearing off the boy before his eyes, scarcely ten feet distant, he could not, despite his gigantic efforts, overtake the drowning child. On flew the youth and child, and it was miraculous how each escaped being dashed in pieces against the rocks. Twice the boy went out of sight, and a suppressed shriek escaped the mother's lips; but twice he reappeared, and with hands wrung wildly together and breathless anxiety, she followed his progress as his unresisting form was hurried with the onward current.

The youth now appeared to redouble his exertions, for they were approaching the most dangerous part of the river, where the rapids, contracting between the narrow shores, shot almost perpendicularly down a declivity of fifteen feet. The rush of the waters at this spot was tremendous, and no one ventured to approach its vicinity, even in a canoe, lest he should be dashed in pieces. What, then, would be the youth's fate, unless he soon overtook the child? He seemed fully sensible of the increasing peril and now urged his way through the foaming current with a desperate strength.

Three times he was on the point of grasping the child, when the waters whirled the prize from him. The third effort was made just as they were entering within the influence of the current above the fall; and when it failed, the mother's heart sunk within her, and she groaned, fully expecting the youth to give up his task. But no, he only pressed forward the more eagerly; and, as they breathlessly watched amid the boiling waters, they saw the form of the brave youth following close after that of the boy.

And now, like an arrow from the bow, pursuer and pursued shot to the brink of the precipice. An instant they hung there, distinctly visible amid the foaming waters. Every brain grew dizzy at the sight. But a shout of involuntary exultation burst from the spectators, when they saw the boy held aloft by the right arm of the youth—a shout that was suddenly checked with horror, when they both vanished into the abyss below!

A moment elapsed before a word was spoken or a breath drawn. The mother ran forward and then stood gazing with fixed eyes at the foot of the cataract as if her all depended upon what the next moment should reveal.

Suddenly she gave the glad cry, "There they are! See! They are safe! —Great God, I thank thee!"

And, sure enough, there was the youth still unharmed and still buffeting the waters. He had just emerged from the boiling vortex below the cataract. With one hand, he held aloft the child; with the other, he was making for the shore.

They ran, they shouted, they scarcely knew what they did until they reached his side, just as he was struggling to the bank. They drew him out almost exhausted. The boy was senseless; but his mother declared that he still lived, as she pressed him frantically to her bosom. The youth could scarcely stand, so faint was he from his exertions.

Who can describe the scene that followed—the mother's calmness while she strove to resuscitate her boy and her wild gratitude to his preserver, when the child was out of danger, and sweetly sleeping in her arms? Our pen shrinks at the task. But her words, pronounced then, were remembered afterwards by more than one who heard them.

"God will reward you," said she, "as I can not. He will do great things for you in return for this day's work, and the blessings of thousands besides mine will attend you."

And so it was; for, to the hero of that hour, were subsequently confided the destinies of a mighty nation. But, throughout his long career, what tended to make him more honored and respected beyond all men, was the self-sacrificing spirit, which, in the rescue of that mother's child, as in the more august events of his life, characterized OUR BELOVED WASHINGTON.

Written Summation

Oh, how that mother's straining eyes followed him in his perilous career. How her heart sunk when he went under. And what a gush of joy she felt when she saw him emerging again from the waters, flinging the waves aside with his athletic arms, and struggling on in pursuit of her boy!

Model Practice 1

Model Practice 2

Model Practice 3

Franklin's Wonderful Kite
by James Baldwin

Benjamin Franklin was not only a printer, politician, and statesman, he was the first scientist of America. In the midst of perplexing cares it was his delight to study the laws of nature and try to understand some of the mysteries of creation.

In his time no very great discoveries had yet been made. The steam engine was unknown. The telegraph had not so much as been dreamed about. Thousands of comforts which we now enjoy through the discoveries of science were then unthought of; or if thought of, they were deemed to be impossible.

Franklin began to make experiments in electricity when he was about forty years old.

He was the first person to discover that lightning is caused by electricity. He had long thought that this was true, but he had no means of proving it.

He thought that if he could stand on some high tower during a thunderstorm, he might be able to draw some of the electricity from the clouds through a pointed iron rod. But there was no high tower in Philadelphia. There was not even a tall church spire.

At last he thought of making a kite and sending it up to the clouds. A paper kite, however, would be ruined by the rain and would not fly to any great height.

So instead of paper he used a light silk handkerchief which he fastened to two slender but strong cross pieces. At the top of the kite he placed a pointed iron rod. The string was of hemp, except a short piece at the lower end, which was of silk. At the end of the hemp string an iron key was tied.

"I think that is a queer kind of kite," said Franklin's little boy. "What are you going to do with it?"

"Wait until the next thunder-storm, and you will see," said Franklin. "You may go with me and we will send it up to the clouds."

He told no one else about it, for if the experiment should fail, he did not care to have everybody laugh at him.

At last, one-day, a thunderstorm came up, and Franklin, with his son, went out into a field to fly his kite. There was a steady breeze, and it was easy to send the kite far up towards the clouds.

Then, holding the silken end of the string, Franklin stood under a little shed in the field, and watched to see what would happen.

The lightnings flashed, the thunder rolled, but there was no sign of electricity in the kite. At last, when he was about to give up the experiment, Franklin saw the loose fibers of his hempen string begin to move.

He put his knuckles close to the key, and sparks of fire came flying to his hand. He was wild with delight. The sparks of fire were electricity; he had drawn them from the clouds.

That experiment, if Franklin had only known it, was a very dangerous one. It was fortunate for him, and for the world, that he suffered no harm. More than one person who has since tried to draw electricity from the clouds has been killed by the lightning that has flashed down the hempen kite string.

When Franklin's discovery was made known it caused great excitement among the learned men of Europe. They could not believe it was true until some of them had proved it by similar experiments.

They could hardly believe that a man in the far-away city of Philadelphia could make a discovery which they had never thought of as possible. Indeed, how could an American do anything that was worth doing?

Franklin soon became famous in foreign countries as a philosopher and man of science. The universities of Oxford and Edinburgh honored him by conferring upon him their highest degrees. He was now "Doctor" Benjamin Franklin. But in America people still thought of him only as a man of affairs, as a great printer, and as the editor of Poor Richard's Almanac.

All this happened before the beginning of his career as ambassador from the colonies to the king and government of England.

I cannot tell you of all of his discoveries in science. He invented the lightning rod, and by trying many experiments, he learned more about electricity than the world had ever known before.

He made many curious experiments to discover the laws of heat, light, and sound. By laying strips of colored cloth on snow, he learned which colors are the best conductors of heat.

He invented the harmonica, an ingenious musical instrument, in which the sounds were produced by musical glasses.

During his long stay abroad he did not neglect his scientific studies. He visited many of the greatest scholars of the time, and was everywhere received with much honor.

The great scientific societies of Europe, the Royal Academies in Paris and in Madrid, had already elected him as one of their members. The King of France wrote him a letter, thanking him for his useful discoveries in electricity, and for his invention of the lightning rod.

All this would have made some men very proud. But it was not so with Dr. Franklin. In a letter which he wrote to a friend at the time when these honors were beginning to be showered upon him, he said:

"The pride of man is very differently gratified; and had his Majesty sent me a marshal's staff I think I should scarce have been so proud of it as I am of your esteem."

Written Summation

He put his knuckles close to the key, and sparks of fire came flying to his hand. He was wild with delight. The sparks of fire were electricity; he had drawn them from the clouds.

Model Practice 1

Model Practice 2

Model Practice 3

Grandmother Bear
by Edward Eggleston

The Indians on Lake Superior captured Mr. Alexander Henry when they took Fort Mackinaw. This was during the time of Pontiac's War, which the great chief Pontiac started.

Nearly all the white men in Fort Mackinaw were killed, but an Indian friend named Wawatam paid for his life and saved Mr. Henry. He went to live with Wawatam. He shaved his head, put on the dress of an Indian, and lived and hunted as the Indians did.

One day Mr. Henry saw a very large pine tree that had a trunk six feet in diameter. The bark had been scratched by a bear's claws. Far up on the tree there was a large hole with small branches broken all about.

Mr. Henry looked at the snow, which had no bear tracks in it. He thought that an old bear had climbed up into the tree before the snow fell. Bears sleep nearly all winter and do not even come out to get anything to eat.

Mr. Henry told the Indians about the tree. There was no way of getting up to the bear's hole, and they could not get the bear out except by cutting down the tree. But the Indian women did not believe that the Indians could do it. Their axes were too small to chop down so big a tree.

However, the Indians wanted the bear's oil, which is of great use to them. It serves them for lard, and butter, and many other things. So at the tree they went with their little axes. As many as could stand about the tree worked at a time, and when one rested another chopper took his place. They all worked, men and women, and they chopped all day. When the sun went down, they had chopped about halfway through the tree.

The next morning they began again. They chopped away until the top of the great pine tree began to tremble. Slowly it began to lean; then the tree began to fall. Everybody got far out of the way. It fell down among the other trees with a crash that made the woods roar and lay at last upon the ground.

But no bear came out of the big tree. Mr. Henry began to be afraid that there was no bear there. He thought such a crash was enough to wake up the sleepiest bear in the world. At last the nose of the bear poked out of the hole. Then the head came out. Then came out the great brown body of one of the largest bears in the woods. Mr. Henry shot the bear dead.

Though the Indians kill and eat bears, they are very much afraid of the ghosts of the bears after they are dead. They are more afraid of a bear after it is dead than when it is alive. So, whenever an Indian has killed a bear, he always begs the dead bear's pardon. Each of these Indians, now politely, begged pardon of the bear. The old woman that had adopted Mr. Henry for her son took the bear's head in her hands and kissed it. She called it her grandmother and asked it not to do them any harm. The Indians told the dead bear that a white man had killed it. Of course, the dead bear did not say anything.

Though they called the bear their grandmother, they made haste to take off its skin. They were glad to find that Grandma Bear was very fat. It took two persons to carry home the fat. Four more were loaded with the meat of this nice old relative of theirs.

But still wishing to fool the bear's ghost, they carried the head also to their tent. They put all kinds of silver trinkets on the head and many belts of wampum or shell beads on it. In order to please the ghost of Grandmother Bear still more, they laid the head on a kind of table that they made for it and placed a large quantity of tobacco near its nose.

The next morning a feast was made to please the bear's ghost. The head of the bear was lifted, and a new blanket was spread under it. All the Indians lit their pipes and blew tobacco smoke into the bear's nose. Wawatam made a speech to the bear's spirit. He told it they were very sorry to have to kill their friends. But he said it could not be helped, for if they did not do this, they should starve to death.

The speech being over, the whole party ate heartily of the bear's flesh. After three days they even took down the head itself and put it into the kettle. Thus they ate their grandmother up, but they did it very politely.

Written Summation

Though they called the bear their grandmother, they made haste to take off its skin. They were glad to find that Grandma Bear was very fat. It took two persons to carry home the fat. Four more were loaded with the meat of this nice old relative of theirs.

Model Practice 1

Model Practice 2

Model Practice 3

The Good Reader
from a McGuffey Eclectic Reader

It is told of Frederick the Great, King of Prussia, that, as he was seated one day in his private room, a written petition was brought to him with the request that it should be immediately read. The King had just returned from hunting, and the glare of the sun, or some other cause, had so dazzled his eyes that he found it difficult to make out a single word of the writing.

His private secretary happened to be absent; and the soldier who brought the petition could not read. There was a page, or favorite boy servant, waiting in the hall and upon him the King called. The page was a son of one of the noblemen of the court, but proved to be a very poor reader.

In the first place, he did not articulate distinctly. He huddled his words together in the utterance, as if they were syllables of one long word, which he must get through with as speedily as possible. His pronunciation was bad, and he did not modulate his voice so as to bring out the meaning of what he read. Every sentence was uttered with a dismal monotony of voice as if it did not differ in any respect from that which preceded it.

"Stop!" said the King, impatiently. "Is it an auctioneer's list of goods to be sold that you are hurrying over? Send your companion to me."

Another page who stood at the door now entered, and to him the King gave the petition. The second page began by hemming and clearing his throat in such an affected manner that the King jokingly asked him whether he had not slept in the public garden, with the gate open, the night before.

The second page had a good share of self-conceit, however, and so was not greatly confused by the King's jest. He determined that he would avoid the mistake which his comrade had made. So he commenced reading the petition slowly and with great formality, emphasizing every word, and prolonging the articulation of every syllable.

But his manner was so tedious that the King cried out, "Stop! Are you reciting a lesson in the elementary sounds? Out of the room! But no, stay! Send me that little girl who is sitting there by the fountain."

The girl thus pointed out by the King was a daughter of one of the laborers employed by the royal gardener; and she had come to help her father weed the flowerbeds. It chanced that, like many of the poor people in Prussia, she had received a good education. She was somewhat alarmed when she found herself in the King's presence, but took courage when the King told her that he only wanted her to read for him, as his eyes were weak.

Now, Ernestine (for this was the name of the little girl) was fond of reading aloud, and often many of the neighbors would assemble at her father's house to hear her; those who could not read themselves would come to her, also, with their letters from distant friends or children, and she thus formed the habit of reading various sorts of handwriting promptly and well.

The King gave her the petition, and she rapidly glanced through the opening lines to get some idea of what it was about. As she read, her eyes began to glisten, and her breast to heave.

"What is the matter?" asked the King; "don't you know how to read?"

"Oh, yes! Sire," she replied, addressing him with the title usually applied to him: "I will now read it, if you please."

The two pages were about to leave the room. "Remain," said the King. The little girl began to read the petition. It was from a poor widow, whose only son had been drafted to serve in the army, although his health was delicate and his pursuits had been such as to unfit him for military life. His father had been killed in battle, and the son had a strong desire to become a portrait painter.

The writer told her story in a simple, concise manner, that carried to the heart a belief of its truth; and Ernestine read it with so much feeling, and with an articulation so just, in tones so pure and distinct, that when she had finished, the King, into whose eyes the tears had started, exclaimed, "Oh! Now I understand what it is all about; but I might never have known, certainly I never should have felt, its meaning had I trusted to these young gentlemen, whom I now dismiss from my service for one year, advising them to occupy their time in learning to read."

"As for you, my young lady," continued the King, "I know you will ask no better reward for your trouble than the pleasure of carrying to this poor widow my order for her son's immediate discharge. Let me see whether you can write as well as you can read. Take this pen, and write as I dictate."

He then dictated an order, which Ernestine wrote, and he signed. Calling one of his guards, he bade him go with the girl and see that the order was obeyed.

How much happiness was Ernestine the means of bestowing through her good elocution, united to the happy circumstance that brought it to the knowledge of the King! First, there were her poor neighbors, to whom she could give instruction and entertainment. Then, there was the poor widow who sent the petition, and who not only regained her son, but received through Ernestine an order for him to paint the King's likeness; so that the poor boy soon rose to great distinction, and had more orders than he could attend to. Words could not express his gratitude, and that of his mother, to the little girl.

And Ernestine had, moreover, the satisfaction of aiding her father to rise in the world, so that he became the King's chief gardener. The King did not forget her, but had her well educated at his own expense. As for the two pages, she was indirectly the means of doing them good, also; for, ashamed of their bad reading, they commenced studying in earnest, till they overcame the faults that had offended the King. Both finally rose to distinction, one as a lawyer, and the other as a statesman; and they owed their advancement in life chiefly to their good elocution.

Written Summation

His private secretary happened to be absent; and the soldier who brought the petition could not read. There was a page, or favorite boy servant, waiting in the hall and upon him the King called. The page was a son of one of the noblemen of the court, but proved to be a very poor reader.

Model Practice 1

Model Practice 2

Model Practice 3

The Boston Tea-Party

adapted from John Andrews (adapted from a letter written to a friend in 1773)

In 1773, a ship arrived in the Boston Harbor carrying more than one hundred chests of tea. The people from the town and countryside all agreed that the ship should not be allowed to land. But the agents in charge refused to take the tea back to London. The town bells were rung for a general meeting of the citizens. Printed leaflets were posted calling on ``Friends! Citizens! Countrymen!''

A few days later, a meeting was called of the people of Boston and of all the neighboring towns. At ten o'clock in the morning, five or six thousand people met in the Old South Meeting-House where they all voted THAT THE TEA SHOULD GO OUT OF THE HARBOR THAT AFTERNOON!

A committee, with Mr. Rotch, owner of one of the boats, was sent to the customhouse to demand a clearance. The collector answered that he could not give clearance without the duties first being paid. Mr. Rotch was then sent to ask for a pass from Governor Hutchinson. The governor answered that ``consistent with the rules of government and his duty to the king he could not grant one without they produced a previous clearance from the office.''

That night about two hundred men, members of the Sons of Liberty dressed as Mohawk Indians, arrived on Fort Hill. They were clothed with blankets, muffled heads, and copper-colored faces. Each was armed with a hatchet or axe, and a pair of pistols.

They proceeded two by two to Griffin's Wharf, where three tea-ships lay, each with one hundred and fourteen chests of tea on board. And by nine o'clock in the evening every chest was knocked into pieces and flung over the sides, along with the tea.

Not one was hurt, save Captain Conner, who had ripped up the linings of his coat and waistcoat and had filled them with tea. But, being detected, he was handled pretty roughly. They not only stripped him of his clothes but also gave him a coat of mud, with a severe bruising in the bargain. Nothing but their desire not to make a disturbance prevented him from being tarred and feathered.

After the tea was thrown overboard, all the Indians disappeared in a most marvelous fashion. The next day, if a stranger had walked through the streets of Boston and had seen the calm composure of the people, he would hardly have thought that ten thousand pounds of East India Company's tea had been destroyed the night before.

Written Summation

That night about two hundred men, members of the Sons of Liberty dressed as Mohawk Indians, arrived on Fort Hill. They were clothed with blankets, muffled heads, and copper-colored faces. Each was armed with a hatchet or axe, and a pair of pistols.

Model Pracitce 1

Model Practice 2

Model Practice 3

The Midnight Ride
by Nathaniel Hawthorne

>Listen, my children, and you shall hear
>Of the midnight ride of Paul Revere.
>>Longfellow.

The midnight ride of Paul Revere happened a long time ago when this country was ruled by the king of England.

There were thousands of English soldiers in Boston. The king had sent them there to make the people obey his unjust laws. These soldiers guarded the streets of the town; they would not let any one go out or come in without their leave.

The people did not like this. They said, "We have a right to be free men, but the king treats us as slaves. He makes us pay taxes and gives us nothing in return. He sends soldiers among us to take away our liberty."

The whole country was stirred up. Brave men left their homes and hurried toward Boston.

They said, "We do not wish to fight against the king, but we are free men, and he must not send soldiers to oppress us. If the people of Boston must fight for their liberty, we will help them." These men were not afraid of the king's soldiers. Some of them camped in Charlestown, a village near Boston. From the hills of Charlestown they could watch and see what the king's soldiers were doing.

They wished to be ready to defend themselves, if the soldiers should try to do them harm. For this reason they had bought some powder and stored it at Concord, nearly twenty miles away.

When the king's soldiers heard about this powder, they made up their minds to go out and get it for themselves.

Among the watchers at Charlestown was a brave young man named Paul Revere. He was ready to serve his country in any way that he could.

One day a friend of his who lived in Boston came to see him. He came very quietly and secretly, to escape the soldiers.

"I have something to tell you," he said. "Some of the king's soldiers are going to Concord to get the powder that is there. They are getting ready to start this very night."

"Indeed!" said Paul Revere. "They shall get no powder, if I can help it. I will stir up all the farmers between here and Concord, and those fellows will have a hot time of it. But you must help me."

"I will do all that I can," said his friend.

"Well, then," said Paul Revere, "you must go back to Boston and watch. Watch, and as soon as the soldiers are ready to start, hang a lantern in the tower of the old North Church. If they are to cross the river, hang two. I will be here, ready. As soon as I see the light, I will mount my horse and ride out to give the alarm."

And so it was done.

When night came, Paul Revere was at the riverside with his horse. He looked over toward Boston. He knew where the old North Church stood, but he could not see much in the darkness.

Hour after hour, he stood and watched. The town seemed very still; but now and then, he could hear the beating of a drum or the shouting of some soldier.

The moon rose, and by its light he could see the dim form of the church tower, far away. He heard the clock strike ten. He waited and watched.

The clock struck eleven. He was beginning to feel tired. Perhaps the soldiers had given up their plan.

He walked up and down the riverbank, leading his horse behind him; but he kept his eyes turned always toward the dim, dark spot which he knew was the old North Church.

All at once, a light flashed out from the tower. "Ah! There it is!" he cried. The soldiers had started.

He spoke to his horse. He put his foot in the stirrup. He was ready to mount.

Then another light flashed clear and bright by the side of the first one. The soldiers would cross the river.

Paul Revere sprang into the saddle. As a bird let loose, his horse leaped forward. Away they went.

Away they went through the village street and out upon the country road. "Up! Up! " shouted Paul Revere. "The soldiers are coming! Up! Up! And defend yourselves!"

The cry awoke the farmers; they sprang from their beds and looked out. They could not see the speeding horse, but they heard the clatter of its hoofs far down the road, and they understood the cry, "Up! Up! And defend yourselves!"

"It is the alarm! The redcoats are coming," they said to each other. Then they took their guns, their axes, anything they could find, and hurried out.

So, through the night, Paul Revere rode toward Concord. At every farmhouse and every village he repeated his call.

The alarm quickly spread. Guns were fired. Bells were rung. The people for miles around were roused as though a fire were raging.

The king's soldiers were surprised to find everybody awake along the road. They were angry because their plans had been discovered.

When they reached Concord, they burned the courthouse there.

At Lexington, not far from Concord, there was a sharp fight in which several men were killed. This, in history, is called the Battle of Lexington. It was the beginning of the war called the Revolutionary War. But the king's soldiers did not find the gunpowder. They were glad enough to march back without it. All along the road the farmers were waiting for them. It seemed as if every man in the country was after them. And they did not feel themselves safe until they were once more in Boston.

Written Summation

"Well, then," said Paul Revere, "you must go back to Boston and watch. Watch, and as soon as the soldiers are ready to start, hang a lantern in the tower of the old North Church. If they are to cross the river, hang two. I will be here, ready. As soon as I see the light, I will mount my horse and ride out to give the alarm."

Model Practice 1

Model Practice 2

Model Practice 3

The Young Scout
by James Baldwin

When Andrew Jackson was a little boy he lived with his mother in South Carolina. He was eight years old when he heard about the ride of Paul Revere and the famous fight at Lexington.

It was then that the long war, called the Revolutionary War, began. The king's soldiers were sent into every part of the country. The people called them the British. Some called them "red-coats."

There was much fighting; and several great battles took place between the British and the Americans.

At last Charleston, in South Carolina, was taken by the British. Andrew Jackson was then a tall white-haired boy, thirteen years old.

"I am going to help drive those red-coated British out of the country," he said to his mother.

Then, without another word, he mounted his brother's little farm horse and rode away. He was not old enough to be a soldier, but he could be a scout—and a good scout he was.

He was very tall, as tall as a man. He was not afraid of anything. He was strong and ready for every duty.

One day as he was riding through the woods, some British soldiers saw him. They quickly surrounded him and made him their prisoner.

"Come with us," they said, "and we will teach you that the king's soldiers are not to be trifled with."

They took him to the British camp.

"What is your name, young rebel?" said the British captain.

"Andy Jackson."

"Well, Andy Jackson, get down here and clean the mud from my boots."

Andrew's gray eyes blazed as he stood up straight and proud before the haughty captain.

"Sir," he said, "I am a prisoner of war, and demand to be treated as such."

"You rebel!" shouted the captain. "Down with you, and clean those boots at once."

The slim, tall boy seemed to grow taller, as he answered, "I'll not be the servant of any Englishman that ever lived."

The captain was very angry. He drew his sword to hit the boy with its flat side. Andrew threw out his hand and received an ugly gash across the knuckles.

Some other officers, who had seen the whole affair, cried out to the captain, "Shame! He is a brave boy. He deserves to be treated as a gentleman."

Andrew was not held long as a prisoner. The British soldiers soon returned to Charleston, and he was allowed to go home.

In time, Andrew Jackson became a very great man. He was elected to Congress; he was chosen judge of the Supreme Court of Tennessee; he was appointed general in the army; and lastly he was, for eight years, the president of the United States.

Written Summation

In time, Andrew Jackson became a very great man. He was elected to Congress; he was chosen judge of the Supreme Court of Tennessee; he was appointed general in the army; and lastly he was, for eight years, the president of the United States.

Model Practice 1

Model Practice 2

Model Practice 3

Elizabeth Zane
by Edward Eggleston

On the banks of the Ohio River, near the place where the city of Wheeling now stands, there was once a fort called Fort Henry. This fort was of the kind called a blockhouse, which is a house built of logs made to fit close together. The upper part of the house jutted out beyond the lower, in order that the men in the blockhouse might shoot downwards at the Indians if they should come near the house to set it on fire. Fort Henry was surrounded with a stockade; that is, a fence made by setting posts in the ground close together.

During the Revolutionary War, the Indians in the neighborhood of this fort were fighting on the side of the English. A large number of them came to Fort Henry and tried to take it. All the men that were sent outside of the fort to fight the Indians were either killed or kept from going back. The women and the children of the village, which stood near, had all gone into the fort for safety.

When at last the fiercest attack of the Indians was made, there were only twelve men and boys left inside of the fort. These men and boys had made up their minds to do their best to save the lives of the women and children who were with them. Every man and every boy in the fort knew how to shoot a rifle. They had guns enough, but they had very little powder. So they fired only when they were sure of hitting one of the enemy.

The Indians kept shooting all the time. Some of them crept near the blockhouse, trying to shoot through the cracks, but the bullets of the men inside brought down these brave warriors.

After many hours of fighting, the Indians went off a little way to rest. The white men had now used nearly all their gunpowder. They began to wish for a keg of powder that had been left in one of the houses outside. They knew that whoever should go for this would be seen and fired at by the Indians. He would have to run to the house and back again. The colonel called his men together and told them he did not wish to order any man to do so dangerous a thing as to get the powder, but he said he should like to have some one offer to go for it.

Three or four young men offered to go. The colonel told them he could not spare more than one of them. They must settle among themselves which one should go. But each one of the brave fellows wanted to go, and none of them was willing to give up to another. Then there stepped forward a young woman named Elizabeth Zane.

"Let me go for the powder," she said.

The brave men were surprised. It would be a desperate thing for a man to go. Nobody had dreamed that a woman would venture to do such a thing, nor would any of them agree to let a young woman go into danger.

The colonel said, "No." Her friends begged her not to run the risk. They told her, besides, that any one of the young men could run faster than she could.

But Elizabeth said, "You cannot spare a single man. There are not enough men in the fort now. If I am killed, you will be as strong to fight as before. Let the young men stay where they are needed and let me go for the powder."

She had made up her mind, and nobody could persuade her not to go. So the gate of the fort was opened just wide enough for her to get out. Her friends gave her up to die.

Some of the Indians saw the gate open and saw the young woman running to the house, but they did not shoot at her. They probably thought that they would not waste a bullet on a woman. They could make her a prisoner at any time.

She did not try to carry the powder keg, but she took the powder in a girl's way. She filled her apron with it. When she came out of the house, with her apron full of powder, and started to run back to the fort, the Indians fired at her. It happened that all of their bullets missed her. The gate was opened again, and she got safely into the fort. The men were glad that they had powder enough, and they all felt braver than ever, after they had seen what a girl could do.

The Indians had seen the gate opened to let her out and to let her in again. They thought they could force the gate open; but they could not go and push against it, because the men in the blockhouse would shoot them if they did. So they made a wooden cannon. They got a hollow log and stopped up one end of it. Then they went to the blacksmith's shop in the little village and got some chains. They tied these chains round the log to hold it together. They had no cannon balls, so after putting gunpowder into the log, they put in stones and bits of iron. After dark that evening they dragged this wooden cannon up near to the gate. When all was ready, they touched off their cannon. The log cannon burst into pieces, and killed some of the Indians, but did not hurt the fort.

The next day white men came from other places to help the men in the fort. They got into the fort, and after a few more attacks, the Indians gave up the battle and went away.

Whenever the story of the brave fight at Fort Henry is told, people do not forget that the bravest one in it was the girl that brought her apron full of gunpowder to the men in the fort.

Written Summation

Three or four young men offered to go. The colonel told them he could not spare more than one of them. They must settle among themselves which one should go. But each one of the brave fellows wanted to go, and none of them was willing to give up to another. Then there stepped forward a young woman named Elizabeth Zane.

Model Practice 1

Model Practice 2

Model Practice 3

The Capture of Major Andre
adapted from a Sanders' Union Reader

One of the saddest events in the history of the American Revolution is the treason of Arnold, and in consequence of it, the death of Major Andre. Arnold was an officer in the American army, who, though brave, had a proud and impatient spirit.

He fancied he had not all the honor and the pay due for his services, and having plunged himself into debt by his expensive style of living, these things soured his heart. And, as is the case with ungenerous minds, he never acknowledged a fault nor forgave an injury. More than this, he sought revenge against his countrymen by plotting treason against his country.

Soon after forming this bad design, he opened a secret correspondence with the English General, Henry Clinton, and at the same time, asked General Washington to give him the command of West Point, an important post on the Hudson River. Washington let him have it, and this he determined to betray into the hands of the enemy, provided he could make out of it a good bargain for himself.

He wrote to General Clinton what he would do and asked to have a secret interview with some English officer, in order to agree upon the terms. General Clinton was delighted for he thought an army divided against itself must prove an easy conquest. And he asked Major Andre, a gallant young officer, to meet Arnold and settle the price of his treason.

Andre did not wish to engage in such business; but he obeyed and went up the Hudson in an English sloop-of-war for this purpose. Arnold agreed to meet him at a certain spot and, when night came on, sent a little boat to bring him ashore. He landed at the foot of a mountain called the Long Clove, on the western side of the river, a few miles from Haverstraw, where he found the traitor hid in a clump of bushes.

Little did poor Andre foresee the fatal consequences of this step. All that still starlit night they sat and talked; daylight came, and the business was not concluded. Arnold dismissed the boatmen and led his companion to a solitary farmhouse on the river's bank, where the papers were finally drawn up and hid in one of Andre's stockings. Andre felt how exposed he was to danger in the enemy's country and heartily wished himself back to the sloop.

Forced now, however, to go by land, Arnold gave him a pass to go through the American lines; and at sunset, he set off on horseback with a guide. They crossed the river and, getting along on their dangerous journey with but few alarms, the guide left the next morning, and Andre rode briskly on, congratulating himself upon leaving all dangers behind, for he was rapidly nearing the English lines. When, suddenly, there was a loud shout, "Stand! HALT!" and three men issued from the woods, one seizing the bridle and the others presenting their guns.

Andre told them he had a pass to White Plains on urgent business from General Arnold and begged them not to detain him; but the men, suspecting that all was not right, began to search him; and hauling off his boots, they discovered his papers in his stockings.

Finding himself detected, he offered them any sum of money, if they would let him go. "No;" answered the sturdy men, "not if you would give us ten thousand guineas;" for, though poor, they were above selling their country at any price. Andre was sent a prisoner to General Washington's camp. Arnold, on learning the news of his capture, immediately fled from West Point and made his escape to the English sloop.

According to the rules of war, poor Andre was sentenced to the death of a spy. Great efforts were made to save him. General Clinton offered a large sum to redeem him. So young, so amiable, so gallant, and to meet a felon's doom! But, in ten days he was hung.

Arnold lived; but with the thirty thousand dollars—the price of his treachery—he lived a miserable man, despised even by those who bought him. And one impressive lesson, which the story teaches, is that the consequences of guilt do not fall alone on the guilty man; others are often involved in distress, disgrace, and ruin.

Written Summation

Arnold lived; but with the thirty thousand dollars — the price of his treachery — he lived a miserable man, despised even by those who bought him. And one impressive lesson, which the story teaches, is that the consequences of guilt do not fall alone on the guilty man; others are often involved in distress, disgrace, and ruin.

Model Practice 1

Model Practice 2

Model Practice 3

Webster and the Woodchuck
adapted from a Sanders' Union Reader (adapted from Boston Traveler)

Ebenezer Webster, the father of Daniel, was a farmer. The vegetables in his garden had suffered considerably from the depredations of a woodchuck, which had his hole or habitation near the premises. Daniel, some ten or twelve years old, and his older brother Ezekiel had set a trap and finally succeeded in capturing the trespasser.

Ezekiel proposed to kill the animal and end, at once, all further trouble from him; but Daniel looked with compassion upon his meek, dumb captive and offered to let him again go free. The boys could not agree, and they appealed to their father to decide the case.

"Well, my boys," said the old gentleman, "I will be the judge. There is the prisoner and you shall be the counsel and shall plead the case for and against his life and liberty."

Ezekiel opened the case with a strong argument, urging the mischievous nature of the criminal and the great harm he had already done. He said that much time and labor had been spent in his capture, and now, if he were suffered to live and go again at large, he would renew his depredations and be cunning enough not to suffer himself to be caught again.

He urged, further, that his skin was of some value, and if they were to make the most of him they could, it would not repay half the damage he had already done. His argument was ready, practical, to the point, and of much greater length than our limits will allow us to occupy in relating the story.

The father looked with pride upon his son, who became a distinguished jurist in his manhood. "Now, Daniel, it is your turn. I'll hear what you have to say."

Daniel saw that the plea of his brother had sensibly affected his father, the judge. He, with his large, brilliant, black eyes looked upon the soft, timid expression of the animal and saw it tremble with fear in its narrow prison-house. His heart swelled with pity, and he urged, with eloquent words, that the captive might again go free.

"God," he said, "has made the woodchuck; he made him to live, to enjoy the bright sunlight, the pure air, the free fields and woods. God has not made him, or anything, in vain; the woodchuck has as much right to life as any other living thing."

"He is not a destructive animal, as are the wolf and the fox; he simply ate a few common vegetables, of which we have plenty, and could well spare a part. He destroyed nothing except the little food he needed to sustain his humble life; and that little food was as sweet to him, and as necessary to his existence, as was to us the food upon our mother's table."

"God has furnished us food and has given unto us all that we possess. Could we not spare a little for the dumb creature, that really has as much right to his small share of God's bounty as we ourselves have to our portion?"

"Yea, more, the animal has never violated the laws of his nature nor the laws of God, as man often does; but strictly followed the simple, harmless instincts he has received from the hand of the Creator of all things. Created by God's hand, he has a right—a right from God—to life, to food, to liberty; and we have no right to deprive him of either."

He alluded to the mute, but earnest pleadings of the animal for that life, as sweet and as dear to him, as their own was to them. And the just judgment they might expect, if, in selfish cruelty and cold heartlessness, they took the life they could not restore—the life that God alone had given.

During this appeal, the tears had started to the old man's eyes and were fast running down his sunburned cheeks. Every feeling of a father's heart was stirred within him. He saw the future greatness of his son before his eyes and felt that God had blessed him in his children, beyond the lot of most men.

His pity and sympathy were awakened by the eloquent words of compassion and the strong appeal for mercy. Forgetting the judge in the man and father, he sprang from his chair, while Daniel was in the midst of his argument, without thinking he had already won his case, and turning to his older son, dashing the tears from his eyes, exclaimed, "Ezekiel, Ezekiel, you let that woodchuck go!"

Written Summation

During this appeal, the tears had started to the old man's eyes and were fast running down his sunburned cheeks. Every feeling of a father's heart was stirred within him. He saw the future greatness of his son before his eyes and felt that God had blessed him in his children, beyond the lot of most men.

Model Practice 1

Model Practice 2

Model Practice 3

Benedict Arnold
from a Sanders' Union Reader

There was a day when Talleyrand arrived in Havre, direct from Paris. It was the darkest hour of the French Revolution. Pursued by the bloodhounds of the Reign of Terror, stripped of every wreck of property or power, Talleyrand secured a passage to America aboard a ship about to sail. He was a beggar and a wanderer in a strange land, looking to earn his bread by daily labor.

"Is there an American staying at your house?" he asked the landlord of the hotel. "I am bound to cross the water and should like a letter to a person of influence in the New World."

The landlord hesitated a moment then replied, "There is a gentleman upstairs, either from America or Britain; but whether an American or an Englishman, I can not tell."

He pointed the way, and Talleyrand, who, in his life, was Bishop, Prince, and Prime Minister, ascended the stairs. A miserable suppliant, he stood before the stranger's door, knocked, and entered. In the far corner of the dimly lit room sat a man of some fifty years, his arms folded and his head bowed on his breast. From a window directly opposite, a faint light rested on his forehead.

His eyes looked from beneath the downcast brows and gazed on Talleyrand's face with a peculiar and searching expression. His face was striking in outline, the mouth and chin indicative of an iron will. His form, vigorous, even with the snows of fifty winters, was clad in a dark but rich and distinguished costume.

Talleyrand advanced, stated that he was a fugitive; and, under the impression that the gentleman before him was an American, he solicited his kind and generous offices. He related his history in eloquent French and broken English.

"I am a wanderer and an exile. I am forced to flee to the New World without a friend or home. You are an American! Give me, then, I beseech you, a letter of yours, so that I may be able to earn my bread. I am willing to toil in any manner; the scenes of Paris have seized me with such horror, that a life of labor would be a paradise to a career of luxury in France. You will give me a letter to one of your friends? A gentleman like yourself has, doubtless, many friends."

The strange gentleman rose. With a look that Talleyrand never forgot, he retreated to the door of the next chamber, his eyes looking still from beneath his darkened brow. He spoke as he retreated backward; his voice was full of meaning.

"I am the only man born in the New World who can raise his hand to God and say I have not a friend, not one, in all America!"

Talleyrand never forgot the overwhelming sadness of that look which accompanied these words.

"Who are you?" he cried, as the strange man retreated to the next room, "your name?"

"My name," he replied, with a smile that had more of mockery than joy in its convulsive expression—"my name is Benedict Arnold!"

He was gone: Talleyrand sank into his chair, gasping the words, "ARNOLD, THE TRAITOR!"

Thus, you see, he wandered over the earth another Cain, with the wanderer's mark upon his brow. Even in that secluded room, in that inn at Havre, his crimes found him out and forced him to tell his name, that name, the synonym of infamy. The last twenty years of his life are covered with a cloud, from whose darkness but a few gleams of light flash out upon the page of history.

The manner of his death is not exactly known; but we can not doubt that he died utterly friendless remorse pursuing him to the grave, whispering "John Andre" in his ear, and murmuring forever, "True to your country, what might you have been, O ARNOLD, THE TRAITOR!"

Written Summation

There was a day when Talleyrand arrived in Havre, direct from Paris. It was the darkest hour of the French Revolution. Pursued by the bloodhounds of the Reign of Terror, stripped of every wreck of property or power, Talleyrand secured a passage to America aboard a ship about to sail. He was a beggar and a wanderer in a strange land, looking to earn his bread by daily labor.

Model Practice 1

Model Practice 2

Model Practice 3

Old Johnny Appleseed
by Elizabeth Harrison

Many years ago on the sparsely settled prairies of America there lived an old man who was known by the queer name of "Johnny Appleseed." His wife had died long ago and his children had grown up and scattered to the corners of the earth. He had not even a home that he could call his own, but wandered about from place to place, with only a few friends and little or no money. His face was wrinkled, his hair was thin and gray, and his shoulders stooped. His clothes were old and ragged, and his hat was old and shabby. Yet inside of him was a heart that was brave and true, and he felt that even he, old and poor as he was, could be of use in the world, because he loved his fellow-men and love always finds something to do.

As he trudged along the lonely road from town to town or made for himself a path through the unbroken forest, he often thought of the good God and of how all men were children of the One Father. Sometimes he would burst out singing the words of a song that he had learned when he was a young man:

>Millions loving, I embrace you,
>All the world this kiss I send!
>Brothers, o'er yon starry tent
>Dwells a God whose love is true!

These words, by the way, are a part of a great poem you may some day read. And they once so stirred the heart of a great musician that he set them to the finest music the world has ever heard. And now the great thought of a loving God and the great music of a loving man comforted the lonely traveler.

The old man wandered about from village to village, which in those days were scattered far apart. At night he usually earned his crust of bread and lodgings by mending the teakettle or wash-boiler of some farmer's wife. Or he earned his meal by soldering on the handle of her tin cup or the knob to her tea-pot, as he always carried in one of his coat pockets a small charcoal stove and a bit of solder. He always carried under his arm or over his shoulder a green baize bag, and when the mending was done he would oftentimes draw out of this green bag an old violin and begin to play. And the farmer as well as his wife and his children would gather around him and listen to his strange music.

Sometimes it was gay and sometimes it was sad, but always sweet. Sometimes he sang words that he himself had written, and sometimes he sang the songs that had been written by the great masters. But mending broken tinware and playing an old violin were not the only things he did to help the world along. As he wandered from place to place he often noticed how rich the soil was, and he would say to himself, "Some day this will be a great country with thousands of people living on this land. And though I shall never see them and they may never read my verses nor hear my name, still I can help them and add some things to their lives."

So whenever a farmer's wife gave him an apple to eat he carefully saved every seed that lay hidden in the heart of the apple. And the next day, as he trudged along, he would stoop down every now and then and plant a few of the seeds, carefully covering them with the rich black soil of the prairie. Then he would look up reverently to the sky and say, "I can but plant the seed, dear Lord, and Thy clouds may water them, but Thou alone can give the increase. Thou only can cause this tiny seed to grow into a tree whose fruit shall feed my fellow-men." Then the God-like love that would fill his heart at such a thought would cause his face to look young again and his eyes to shine as an angel's eyes must shine, and oftentimes he would sing in clear rich tones:

> Millions loving, I embrace you,
> All the world this kiss I send!
> Brothers, o'er yon starry tent
> Dwells a God whose love is true!

And he knew that God dwelt in his heart as well as in the blue sky above.

When the cold winters came and the ground was frozen too hard for him to plant his apple seeds, he still saved them and would often have a small bag full of them by the time that spring returned again. And this is how he came to be called "Old Johnny Appleseed."

Though nobody took very much notice of what he was doing, he still continued each day to plant apple seeds and each evening to play on his violin.

By-and-by his step grew slower and his shoulders drooped lower until at last his soul, which had always been strong and beautiful, passed out of his worn old body into the life beyond. The cast-off body was buried by some villagers who felt kindly towards the old man but never dreamed that he had ever done any real service for them nor their children. And soon his very name was forgotten. But the tiny apple seeds took root and began to grow; each summer the young saplings grew taller; and each winter they grew stronger until, at last, they were old enough to bear apples. As people moved from the east out to the wild western prairies they naturally enough selected sites for building their homes near the fruitful apple trees. And in the springtime the young men gathered the blossoms for the young maidens to wear in their hair, and in the autumn the fathers gathered the ripe red and yellow apples to store away in their cellars for winter use. The mothers made applesauce and apple pies and apple dumplings of them, and all the year round the little children played under the shade of the apple trees. But none of them ever once thought of the old man who had planted for people he did not know, and who could never even be thanked for his loving services.

Each apple that ripened bore in its heart a number of new seeds; some of which were planted and grew into fine orchards from which were gathered many barrels of apples. These were shipped farther west until the Rocky Mountains were reached. In the center of each apple shipped were more seeds, from which grew more apple trees, which bore the same kind of apples that the wrinkled old man in the shabby old clothes had planted many years before. So that many thousands of people have already benefited from what the poor old man in the shabby old coat did, and thousands yet to come will enjoy the fruits of his labor.

It is true he never wore the armor of a great knight and never held the title of a great general. He never discovered a new world nor helped his favorite to sit on the throne of a king. But perhaps after all, though ragged and poor, he was a hero, because in his heart he really and truly sang, as well as with his lips:

> Millions loving, I embrace you,
> All the world this kiss I send!
> Brothers, o'er yon starry tent
> Dwells a God whose love is true!

For the greatest of all victories is to learn to love others even when they do not know it. This is to be God-like, and to be God-like is to be the greatest of heroes.

Written Summation

In the springtime the young men gathered the blossoms for the young maidens to wear in their hair, and in the autumn the fathers gathered the ripe red and yellow apples to store away in their cellars for winter use. The mothers made applesauce and apple pies and apple dumplings of them, and all the year round the little children played under the shade of the apple trees.

Model Practice 1

Model Practice 2

Model Practice 3

Napoleon's Army Crossing the Alps
from a Sanders' Union Reader

When Napoleon was carrying war into Italy, he ordered one of his officers, Marshal Macdonald, to cross the Splugen with fifteen thousand soldiers and join him on the plains below. The Splugen is one of the four great roads which cross the Alps from Switzerland to Italy.

When Macdonald received the order, it was about the last of November, and the winter storms were raging among the mountain passes. It was a perilous undertaking, yet he must obey; and the men began their terrible march through narrow defiles and overhanging precipices, six thousand feet up, up among the gloomy solitude of the Alps.

The cannon were placed on sleds drawn by oxen, and the ammunition was packed on mules. First came the guides, sticking their long poles in the snow, in order to find the path; then came workmen to clear away the drifts; then the dragoons, mounted on their most powerful horses, to beat down the track; after which followed the main body of the army.

They encountered severe storms and piercing cold. When halfway up the summit, a rumbling noise was heard among the cliffs. The guides looked at each other in alarm for they knew well what it meant. It grew louder and louder. "An avalanche! An avalanche!" they shrieked, and the next moment a field of ice and snow came leaping down the mountain, striking the line of march, and sweeping thirty dragoons in a wild plunge below. The black forms of the horses and their riders were seen for an instant struggling for life, and then they disappeared forever.

The sight struck the soldiers with horror; they crouched and shivered in the blast. Their enemy was not now flesh and blood but wild winter storms; swords and bayonets could not defend them from the desolating avalanche. Flight or retreat was hopeless, for all around lay the drifted snow, like a vast winding-sheet. On they must go, or death was certain, and the brave men struggled forward.

"Soldiers!" exclaimed their commander, "you are called to Italy; your general needs you. Advance and conquer, first the mountain and the snow then the plains and the enemy!" Blinded by the winds, benumbed with the cold and far beyond the reach of aid, Macdonald and his men pressed on. Sometimes a whole company of soldiers was suddenly swept away by an avalanche.

On one occasion, a poor drummer, crawling out from the mass of snow, which had torn him from his comrades, began to beat his drum for relief. The muffled sound came up from his gloomy resting-place and was heard by his brother soldiers, but none could go to his rescue. For an hour, he beat rapidly; then the strokes grew fainter, until they were heard no more, and the poor drummer laid himself down to die. Two weeks were occupied in this perilous march, and two hundred men perished in the undertaking.

This passage of the Splugen is one of the bravest exploits in the history of Napoleon's generals, and illustrates the truth of the proverb, "Where there is a will there is a way." No one can read the heroic deeds of brave men grappling with danger and death without a feeling of respect and admiration; but heroic deeds are always the fruit of toil and self-sacrifice. No one can accomplish great things unless he aims at great things and pursues that aim with unflinching courage and perseverance.

Written Summation

When halfway up the summit, a rumbling noise was heard among the cliffs. The guides looked at each other in alarm for they knew well what it meant. It grew louder and louder. "An avalanche! An avalanche!" they shrieked, and the next moment a field of ice and snow came leaping down the mountain, striking the line of march, and sweeping thirty dragoons in a wild plunge below.

Model Practice 1

Model Practice 2

Model Practice 3

A Foot Race for Life
by Edward Eggleston

In 1803 that part of our country which lies west of the Mississippi was almost unknown to the white men. In that year the President sent Captain Lewis and Captain Clark to see what the country was like. They went up the Missouri River and across the Rocky Mountains. Then they went down the Columbia River to the Pacific Ocean. It took them more than two years to make the trip there and back.

Lewis and Clark had about forty-five men with them. One of these men was named Colter. In the very heart of the wild country he left the party and set up as a trapper. A trapper is a man who catches animals in traps in order to get their skins to sell. The Blackfoot Indians made Colter a prisoner. Colter knew a little of their language. He heard them talking of how they should kill their prisoner. They thought it would be fun to set him up and shoot at him with their arrows until he was dead. At this time the Indians on the western plains had no guns. But the Indian chief thought he knew a better way. He laid hold of Colter's shoulder, and said,

"Can you run fast?"

Colter could run very swiftly, but he pretended to the chief that he was a bad runner. So they took him out on the prairie about four hundred yards away from the Indians. There he was turned loose and told to run.

The whole band of Indians ran after him, yelling like wild beasts. Colter did not look back. He had to run through thorns that hurt his bare feet, but he was running for his life. Six miles away there was a river. If he could get to that, he might escape.

He almost flew over the ground. At first he did not turn his head round; however, when he had run about three miles, he glanced back. He saw that most of the Indians had lost ground, but the best runners were ahead of the others. One Indian, swifter than all the rest, was only about a hundred yards behind him. This man had a spear in his hand, ready to kill Colter as soon as he should be near enough.

Poor Colter now ran harder than ever to get away from this Indian. At last he was only about a mile from the river. He looked back and saw the swift Indian only twenty yards away, with his spear ready to throw.

It was of no use for Colter to keep on running. He turned around and faced the swift runner, who was about to throw his spear. Colter spread his arms wide and stood still.

The Indian was surprised at this. He tried to stop running, so as to kill the white man with his spear. But he had already run himself nearly to death, and when he tried to stop quickly, he lost his balance and fell forward to the ground. His lance stuck in the earth and broke in two.

Colter quickly pulled the pointed end of the spear out of the ground and killed the fallen Indian. Then he turned and ran on toward the river.

The other Indians were coming swiftly behind; but, as they passed the place where the first one lay dead, each of them stopped a moment to howl over him, after their custom. This gave Colter a little more time. He ran through a patch of woods, jumped in the river, and swam toward a little island. Logs and brush had floated down the river and lodged across the island. This driftwood had formed a great raft. Colter dove under this raft and swam to a place where he could push his head up to get air and still remain hidden by the brush.

The Indians were already yelling on the bank of the river. A moment later they were swimming toward the island. When they reached the drift pile, they ran this way and that. They looked into all the cracks trying to find the white man. They ran right over his hiding place. Colter thought they would surely find him.

But after a long time they went away. Colter thought they would set fire to the raft of driftwood, but they did not think of that. Perhaps they thought that Colter had drowned.

He lay still under the raft till night came. Then he swam down the stream a long distance, left the water, and went far out on the prairie. Here he felt safe from his enemies.

But he had no clothes and no food. He had no gun to shoot animals with, and it was several days' journey to the nearest place where there were white men, a trading house.

Colter had nothing to eat but roots. The sun burned his skin in the daytime, and he shivered without a covering at night. The thorns hurt his feet as he walked, but he found his way to the trading house at last.

He used to tell of wonderful things that he saw while traveling to the trading house. He saw springs that were boiling hot and steaming. He saw fountains that would sometimes spout hot water into the air for hundreds of feet.

He used to tell of these and many other wonderful things that he saw. But nobody believed his stories. Nobody had ever seen anything of the kind in this country. When Colter would tell of these things, those who heard him thought that he was making up stories or that he had been out of his head while traveling and had imagined such wonders.

But after many long years the wonderful place, which we call Yellowstone Park, was found, and in it were boiling and spouting springs. People knew then that Colter had been telling the truth and that he had traveled through the Yellowstone country.

Written Summation

He almost flew over the ground. At first he did not turn his head round; however, when he had run about three miles, he glanced back. He saw that most of the Indians had lost ground, but the best runners were ahead of the others. One Indian, swifter than all the rest, was only about a hundred yards behind him. This man had a spear in his hand, ready to kill Colter as soon as he should be near enough.

Model Practice 1

Model Practice 2

Model Practice 3

The Rescue
adapted from a Sanders' Union Reader (by a Sea Captain)

On a bright moonlight night, in the month of February 1831, when it was intensely cold, the little brig, which I commanded, lay quietly at her anchors inside of Sandy Hook. We had had a hard time, beating about for eleven days off this coast, with cutting north-easters blowing and snow and sleet falling for the most part of that time.

Forward, the vessel was thickly coated with ice, and it was hard work to handle her, as the rigging and sails were stiff and yielded only when the strength of the men was exerted to the utmost. When we, at length, made the port, all hands were worn down and exhausted.

"A bitter cold night, Mr. Larkin," I said to my mate, as I tarried for a short time upon deck.

The worthy down-easter caused him to button his coat more tightly around him, and looking up to the moon, he replied, "It's a whistler, captain. Nothing can live comfortably out of blankets tonight."

"The tide is running out swift and strong, and it will be well to keep a sharp lookout for this floating ice, Mr. Larkin," I said as I turned to go below.

"Ay, ay, sir," responded the faithful mate.

About two hours afterward, I was aroused from a sound sleep by the vigilant officer.

"Excuse me for disturbing you, captain," he said, detecting an expression of vexation in my face, "but I wish you would turn out, and come on deck as soon as possible."

"What's the matter, Mr. Larkin?" I asked.

"Why, sir, I have been watching a large cake of ice which swept by, at a distance, a moment ago; and I saw something black upon it, something that I thought moved. The moon is under a cloud, and I could not see distinctly; but I believe there is a child floating out to the sea this freezing night on that cake of ice."

We were on deck before either spoke another word. The mate pointed out, with no little difficulty, the cake of ice floating off to the leeward with its white glittering surface broken by a black spot.

"Get the glass, Mr. Larkin," I ordered. "The moon will be out of that cloud in a moment, and then we can see distinctly."

I kept my eye upon the receding mass of ice, while the moon was slowly working her way through a heavy bank of clouds. The mate stood by me with the glass. And when the full light fell upon the water, with brilliance only known in our northern latitudes, I put the glass to my eye. One glance was enough.

"Forward, there!" I hailed at the top of my voice. With one bound, I reached the main hatch and began to clear away the little cutter, which was stowed in the ship's yawl.

Mr. Larkin had taken the glass to look for himself, "There are two children on that cake of ice!" he exclaimed as he hastened to assist me in getting out the boat.

The men answered my hail and walked quickly aft. In a short space of time, we launched the cutter, into which Mr. Larkin and myself jumped, followed by the two men who took the oars. I rigged the tiller, and the mate sat beside me in the stern sheets.

"Do you see that cake of ice with something black upon it, my lads? Put me alongside of that, and I'll give you a month's extra wages when you are paid off," I challenged them.

They bent to their oars, but their strokes were uneven and feeble, for they were worn out by the hard duty of the preceding fortnight. And, though they did their best, the boat made little more headway than the tide.

It was a losing chase.

Mr. Larkin, who was suffering torture as he saw how little we gained, cried out, "Pull, lads! I'll double the captain's prize, two months' extra pay. Pull lads! Pull for life!"

A convulsive effort at the oars told how willing the men were to obey, but the strength of the strong man was gone. One of the poor fellows washed us twice in recovering his oar and then gave out; and the other was nearly as far gone.

Mr. Larkin sprang forward and seized the deserted oar. "Lie down in the bottom of the boat," he said to the man; "and, captain, take the other oar; we must row for ourselves."

I took the second man's place. Larkin had stripped off his coat, and as he pulled the bow, I waited for the signal stroke. It came gently, but firmly; and the next moment we were pulling a long, steady stroke, gradually increasing in rapidity until the wood seemed to smoke in the row-locks. We kept time, each by the long, deep breathing of the other.

Such a pull! We bent forward until our faces almost touched our knees; and then, throwing all our strength into the backward movement drew on the oar until every inch covered by the sweep was gained. Thus we worked at the oars for fifteen minutes, and it seemed to me as many hours. The sweat rolled off in great drops, and I was enveloped in a steam generated from my own body.

"Are we almost up to it, Mr. Larkin?" I gasped out.

"Almost, captain," he answered. "And don't give up! For the love of our dear little ones at home, don't give up, captain!"

The oars flashed as their blades turned up to the moonlight, for the men who plied them were fathers and had fathers' hearts.

Suddenly Mr. Larkin ceased pulling, and my heart, for a moment, almost stopped its beating. For the terrible thought that he had given out crossed my mind, but I was reassured by his voice.

"Gently, captain, gently, a stroke or two more, there, that will do." And the next moment Mr. Larkin sprang upon the ice. Calling to the men to fasten the boat to the ice, I started up and followed him.

We ran to the dark spot in the center of the mass and found two little boys. The head of the smaller was resting in the bosom of the larger; both were fast asleep. The lethargy, which would have been fatal except for the timely rescue, had overcome them.

Mr. Larkin grasped one of the lads, cut off his shoes, tore off his jacket, and then, loosening his own garments to the skin, placed the cold child in contact with his own warm body, carefully wrapping his overcoat around him. I did the same with the other child, and we then returned to the boat.

The children, as we learned when we had the delight of restoring them to their parents, were playing on the cake of ice, which had jammed into a bend of the river, about ten miles above New York. A movement of the tide set the ice in motion, and the little fellows were borne away, that cold night, and would have inevitably perished, but for Mr. Larkin's espying them as they were sweeping out to sea.

"How do you feel, Mr. Larkin?" I said to the mate the morning after this adventure.

"A little stiff in the arms, captain," the noble fellow replied, while the big tears of grateful happiness gathered in his eyes. "A little stiff in the arms, captain, but very easy here," laying his hand on the rough chest in which beat a true and manly heart.

He who lashes the seas into fury and lets loose the tempest will care for thee! The storms may rage without, but in thy bosom, peace and sunshine abide always.

Written Summation

Such a pull! We bent forward until our faces almost touched our knees; and then throwing all our strength into the backward movement, drew on the oar until every inch covered by the sweep was gained. Thus we worked at the oars for fifteen minutes, and it seemed to me as many hours. The sweat rolled off in great drops, and I was enveloped in a steam generated from my own body.

Model Practice 1

Model Practice 2

Model Practice 3

The Whisperers
by James Baldwin

"Boys, what did I tell you?"

The schoolmaster spoke angrily. He was in trouble because his scholars would not study. Whenever his back was turned, they were sure to begin whispering to one another.

"Girls, stop your whispering, I say."

But still they would whisper, and he could not prevent it. The afternoon was half-gone, and the trouble was growing. Then the master thought of a plan.

"Children," he said, "we are going to play a new game. The next one that whispers must come out and stand in the middle of the floor. He must stand there until he sees some one else whisper. Then he will tell me, and the one whom he names must come and take his place. He, in turn, will watch and report the first one that he sees whisper. And so we will keep the game going till it is time for school to be dismissed. The boy or girl who is standing at that time will be punished for all of you."

"What will the punishment be, Mr. Johnson?" asked a bold, bad boy. "A good thrashing," answered the master. He was tired; he was vexed; he hardly knew what he said.

The children thought the new game was very funny. First, Tommy Jones whispered to Billy Brown and was at once called out to stand on the floor. Within less than two minutes, Billy saw Mary Green whispering, and she had to take his place. Mary looked around and saw Samuel Miller asking his neighbor for a pencil, and Samuel was called. And so the fun went on until the clock showed that it lacked only ten minutes till school would be dismissed.

Then all became very good and very careful, for no one wished to be standing at the time of dismissal. They knew that the master would be as good as his word. The clock ticked loudly, and Tommy Jones, who was standing up for the fourth time, began to feel very uneasy. He stood on one leg and then on the other and watched very closely; but nobody whispered. Could it be possible that he would receive that thrashing? Suddenly, to his great joy he saw little Lucy Martin lean over her desk and whisper to the girl in front of her. Now Lucy was the pet of the school. Everybody loved her, and this was the first time she had whispered that day. But Tommy didn't care for that. He wished to escape the punishment, and so he called out, "Lucy Martin!" and went proudly to his seat.

Little Lucy had not meant to whisper. There was something which she wished very much to know before going home, and so, without thinking, she had leaned over and whispered just three little words. With tears in her eyes she went out and stood in the whisperer's place.

She was very much ashamed and hurt, for it was the first time that she had ever been in disgrace at school. The other girls felt sorry that she should suffer for so small a fault. The boys looked at her and wondered if the master would really be as good as his word.

The clock kept on ticking. It lacked only one minute till the bell would strike the time for dismissal. What a shame that dear, gentle Lucy should be punished for all those unruly boys and girls!

Then, suddenly, an awkward half-grown boy who sat right in front of the master's desk turned squarely around and whispered to Tommy Jones, three desks away.

Everybody saw him. Little Lucy Martin saw him through her tears but said nothing. Everybody was astonished; for that boy was the best scholar in the school; and he had never been known to break a rule.

It lacked only half a minute now. The awkward boy turned again and whispered so loudly that even the master could not help hearing:

"Tommy, you deserve a thrashing!"

"Elihu Burritt, take your place on the floor," said the master sternly.

The awkward boy stepped out quickly, and little Lucy Martin returned to her seat sobbing. At the same moment the bell struck and school was dismissed.

After all the others had gone home, the master took down his long birch rod and said:

"Elihu, I suppose I must be as good as my word. But tell me why you so deliberately broke the rule against whispering."

"I did it to save little Lucy," said the awkward boy, standing up very straight and brave. "I could not bear to see her punished."

"Elihu, you may go home," said the master.

All this happened many years ago in New Britain, Connecticut. Elihu Burritt was a poor boy who was determined to learn. He worked many years as a blacksmith and studied books whenever he had a spare moment. He learned many languages and became known all over the world as "The Learned Blacksmith."

Written Summation

The children thought the new game was very funny. First, Tommy Jones whispered to Billy Brown and was at once called out to stand on the floor. Within less than two minutes, Billy saw Mary Green whispering, and she had to take his place. Mary looked around and saw Samuel Miller asking his neighbor for a pencil, and Samuel was called. And so the fun went on until the clock showed that it lacked only ten minutes till school would be dismissed.

Model Practice 1

Model Practice 2

Model Practice 3

Finding Gold in California
by Edward Eggleston

    California belonged to Mexico until the Mexican American War. During that war the United States took California away from Mexico. It is now one of the richest and most beautiful States in the Union. In the old days, when California belonged to Mexico, it was a quiet country. Nearly all the white people spoke Spanish, which is the language of Mexico. They lived mostly by raising cattle. In those days people did not know that there was gold in California. A little gold had been found in the southern part of the State, but nobody expected to find valuable gold mines. A few people from the United States had settled in the country. They also raised cattle.

    Sometime after the United States had taken California, peace was made with Mexico. California then became a part of our country. About the time that peace was made, something happened which brought great excitement to the country. It changed the history of our country and changed the business of the whole world. Here is that story:

    A man named Sutter had moved from Missouri to California. He built a house, which was called Sutter's Fort. It was where the city of Sacramento now stands. Sutter had many horses and oxen, and he owned thousands of acres of land. He traded with the Indians and carried on other kinds of business.

    But everything was done the old way. When he wanted boards, he sent men to saw them out by hand. It took two men a whole day to saw up a log to make a dozen boards. There was no sawmill in all California.

    When Sutter wanted to grind flour or meal, this also was done the old way. A large stone roller was run over a flat stone. But at last Sutter thought he would have a grinding mill. To build this, he needed boards. He thought he would first build a sawmill. Then he could get boards quickly for his grinding mill and have lumber to use for other things.

    Sutter sent a man named Marshall to build his sawmill. It was to be built forty miles away from Sutter's Fort because the mill had to be where there were trees to saw.

    Marshall was a very good carpenter, who could build almost anything. He had some men working with him. After some months they finished the mill which was built to run by water.

    But when he started it, the mill did not run well. Marshall saw that he must dig a ditch below the great water wheel to carry off the water. He hired Indians to dig the ditch.

    When the Indians had partly dug this ditch, Marshall went out one January morning to look at it. The clear water was running through the ditch. It had washed away the sand, leaving the pebble exposed. At the bottom of the water Marshall saw the pebble which looked like brass. He put his hand down into the water and took up this bright, yellow pebble. It was about the size and shape of a small pea. Then he looked and found another pretty little yellow pebble at the bottom of the ditch.

    Marshall trembled all over. It might be gold. But he remembered that there is another yellow substance that looks like gold, which is called fool's gold. He was afraid he had only found fool's gold.

    Marshall knew that if it were gold it would not break easily. He laid one of the pieces on a stone; then he took another stone and hammered it. It was soft and did not break. If it had broken to pieces, Marshall would have known that it was not gold.

    In a few days the men had dug up about three ounces of the yellow stuff. They had no means of making sure it was gold.

    Then Marshall got on a horse and set out for Sutter's Fort, carrying the yellow metal with him. He traveled as fast as the rough road would let him. He rode up to Sutter's in the evening, all spattered with mud.

He told Captain Sutter that he wished to see him alone. Marshall's eyes looked wild, and Sutter was afraid that he was crazy but went to a room with him. Then Marshall wanted the door locked. Sutter could not think what was the matter with the man.

When he was sure that nobody else would come in, Marshall poured the little yellow beads that he had brought onto the table.

Sutter thought it was gold, but the men did not know how to tell whether it was pure or not. At last they hunted up a book that told how heavy gold is. Then they got a pair of scales and weighed the gold, putting silver dollars in the other end of the scales for weights. Then they held one end of the scales under water and weighed the gold. By finding how much lighter it was in the water than out of the water, they found that it was pure gold.

All the men at the mill promised to keep the secret. They were all digging up gold when not working in the mill. As soon as the mill should be done, they were going to wash gold.

But the secret could not be kept. A teamster who came to the mill was told about it. He got a few grains of the precious gold.

When the teamster got back to Sutter's Fort, he went to a store to buy a bottle of whisky, but he had no money. The storekeeper would not sell anything to him without money. The teamster then took out some grains of gold. The storekeeper was surprised. He let the man have what he wanted. The teamster would not tell where he got the gold. But after he had taken two or three drinks of the whisky, he was not able to keep his secret. He soon told all he knew about the finding of gold at Sutter's Mill.

The news spread like fire in dry grass. Men rushed to the mill in the mountains to find gold. Gold was also found at other places. Merchants in the towns of California left their stores. Mechanics laid down their tools, and farmers left their fields, to dig gold. Some became rich in a few weeks; others were not so lucky.

Soon the news went across the continent. It traveled also to other countries. More than one hundred thousand men went to California the first year after gold was found, and still more men poured in the next year. Thousands of men went through the Indian country with wagons; there were no railroads to the west in that day.

Millions and millions of dollars' worth of gold was dug. In a short time California became a rich State. Railroads were built across the country. Ships sailed on the Pacific Ocean to carry on the trade of this great State. Every nation of the earth had gold from California.

And it all started from one little, round, yellow bead of gold that happened to lie shining at the bottom of a ditch, on a cold morning not so very long ago.

Written Summation

When the Indians had partly dug this ditch, Marshall went out one January morning to look at it. The clear water was running through the ditch. It had washed away the sand, leaving the pebble exposed. At the bottom of the water Marshall saw the pebble which looked like brass. He put his hand down into the water and took up this bright, yellow pebble.

Model Practice 1

Model Practice 2

Model Practice 3

CHAPTER II

Text Excerpts from Primary Source Documents

The Mayflower Compact
November 11, 1620

In the name of God, Amen. We, whose names are underwritten, the Loyal Subjects of our dread Sovereign Lord, King James, by the Grace of God, of Great Britain, France, and Ireland, King, Defender of the Faith, c.

Having undertaken for the Glory of God, and Advancement of the Christian Faith, and the Honor of our King and Country, a Voyage to plant the first colony in the Northern Parts of Virginia; do, by these Presents, solemnly and mutually in the Presence of God and one of another, covenant and combine ourselves together into a civil Body Politick, for our better Ordering and Preservation, and Furtherance of the Ends aforesaid; And by Virtue hereof do enact, constitute, and frame, such just and equal Laws, Ordinances, Acts, Constitutions, and Offices, from time to time, as shall be thought most meet and convenient for the General Good of the Colony; unto which we promise all due Submission and Obedience.

In Witness whereof we have hereunto subscribed our names at Cape Cod the eleventh of November, in the Reign of our Sovereign Lord, King James of England, France, and Ireland, the eighteenth, and of Scotland, the fifty-fourth, Anno. Domini, 1620.

Mr. John Carver	Mr. Stephen Hopkins
Mr. William Bradford	Digery Priest
Mr. Edward Winslow	Thomas Williams
Mr. William Brewster	Gilbert Winslow
Isaac Allerton	Edmund Margesson
Miles Standish	Peter Brown
John Alden	Richard Bitteridge
John Turner	George Soule
Francis Eaton	Edward Tilly
James Chilton	John Tilly
John Craxton	Francis Cooke
John Billington	Thomas Rogers
Joses Fletcher	Thomas Tinker
John Goodman	John Ridgate
Mr. Samuel Fuller	Edward Fuller
Mr. Christopher Martin	Richard Clark
Mr. William Mullins	Richard Gardiner
Mr. William White	Mr. John Allerton
Mr. Richard Warren	Thomas English
John Howland	Edward Doten

        Edward Liester

Having undertaken for the Glory of God, and Advancement of the Christian Faith, and the Honor of our King and Country, a Voyage to plant the first colony in the Northern Parts of Virginia; do, by these Presents, solemnly and mutually in the Presence of God and one of another, covenant and combine ourselves together into a civil Body Politick, for our better Ordering and Preservation, and Furtherance of the Ends aforesaid.

Model Practice 1

Model Practice 2

Model Practice 3

Benjamin Franklin's 13 Virtues
from Benjamin Franklin's Autobiography

In the various enumerations of the moral virtues I had met with in my reading, I found the catalogue more or less numerous, as different writers included more or fewer ideas under the same name. Temperance, for example, was by some confined to eating and drinking, while by others it was extended to mean the moderating of every other pleasure, appetite, inclination, or passion, bodily or mental, even to our avarice and ambition. I proposed to myself, for the sake of clearness, to use rather more names, with fewer ideas annexed to each, than a few names with more ideas; and I included under thirteen names of virtues all that at that time occurred to me as necessary or desirable, and annexed to each a short precept, which fully expressed the extent I gave to its meaning.

These names of virtues, with their precepts, were:

1. TEMPERANCE. Eat not to dullness; drink not to elevation.

2. SILENCE. Speak not but what may benefit others or yourself; avoid trifling conversation.

3. ORDER. Let all your things have their places; let each part of your business have its time.

4. RESOLUTION. Resolve to perform what you ought; perform without fail what you resolve.

5. FRUGALITY. Make no expense but to do good to others or yourself; i.e., waste nothing.

6. INDUSTRY. Lose no time; be always employed in something useful; cut off all unnecessary actions.

7. SINCERITY. Use no hurtful deceit; think innocently and justly, and if you speak, speak accordingly.

8. JUSTICE. Wrong none by doing injuries, or omitting the benefits that are your duty.

9. MODERATION. Avoid extremes; forbear resenting injuries so much as you think they deserve.

10. CLEANLINESS. Tolerate no uncleanliness in body, cloths, or habitation.

11. TRANQUILLITY. Be not disturbed at trifles, or at accidents common or unavoidable.

12. CHASTITY. Rarely use venery but for health or offspring, never to dullness, weakness, or the injury of your own or another's peace or reputation.

13. HUMILITY. Imitate Jesus and Socrates.

1. Temperance: Eat not to dullness; drink not to elevation.
2. Silence: Speak not but what may benefit others or yourself; avoid trifling conversation.
3. Order: Let all your things have their places; let each part of your business have its time.
4. Resolution: Resolve to perform what you ought; perform without fail what you resolve.
5. Frugality: Make no expense but to do good to others or yourself; i.e., waste nothing.

Model Practice 1

Model Practice 2

Model Practice 3

Give Me Liberty or Give Me Death
by Patrick Henry, March 23, 1775

No man thinks more highly than I do of the patriotism, as well as abilities, of the very worthy gentlemen who have just addressed the House. But different men often see the same subject in different lights; and, therefore, I hope it will not be thought disrespectful to those gentlemen if, entertaining as I do opinions of a character very opposite to theirs, I shall speak forth my sentiments freely and without reserve. This is no time for ceremony. The question before the House is one of awful moment to this country. For my own part, I consider it as nothing less than a question of freedom or slavery; and in proportion to the magnitude of the subject ought to be the freedom of the debate. It is only in this way that we can hope to arrive at truth, and fulfill the great responsibility which we hold to God and our country. Should I keep back my opinions at such a time, through fear of giving offense, I should consider myself as guilty of treason towards my country, and of an act of disloyalty toward the Majesty of Heaven, which I revere above all earthly kings.

Mr. President, it is natural to man to indulge in the illusions of hope. We are apt to shut our eyes against a painful truth, and listen to the song of that siren till she transforms us into beasts. Is this the part of wise men, engaged in a great and arduous struggle for liberty? Are we disposed to be of the number of those who, having eyes, see not, and having ears, hear not, the things which so nearly concern their temporal salvation? For my part, whatever anguish of spirit it may cost, I am willing to know the whole truth; to know the worst, and to provide for it.

I have but one lamp by which my feet are guided, and that is the lamp of experience. I know of no way of judging of the future but by the past. And judging by the past, I wish to know what there has been in the conduct of the British ministry for the last ten years to justify those hopes with which gentlemen have been pleased to solace themselves and the House. Is it that insidious smile with which our petition has been lately received? Trust it not, sir; it will prove a snare to your feet. Suffer not yourselves to be betrayed with a kiss. Ask yourselves how this gracious reception of our petition comports with those warlike preparations which cover our waters and darken our land. Are fleets and armies necessary to a work of love and reconciliation? Have we shown ourselves so unwilling to be reconciled that force must be called in to win back our love? Let us not deceive ourselves, sir. These are the implements of war and subjugation; the last arguments to which kings resort. I ask gentlemen, sir, what means this martial array, if its purpose be not to force us to submission? Can gentlemen assign any other possible motive for it? Has Great Britain any enemy, in this quarter of the world, to call for all this accumulation of navies and armies? No, sir, she has none. They are meant for us: they can be meant for no other. They are sent over to bind and rivet upon us those chains which the British ministry have been so long forging. And what have we to oppose to them? Shall we try argument? Sir, we have been trying that for the last ten years. Have we anything new to offer upon the subject? Nothing. We have held the subject up in every light of which it is capable; but it has been all in vain. Shall we resort to entreaty and humble supplication? What terms shall we find which have not been already exhausted? Let us not, I beseech you, sir, deceive ourselves. Sir, we have done everything that could be done to avert the storm which is now coming on. We have petitioned; we have remonstrated; we have supplicated; we have prostrated ourselves before the throne, and have implored its interposition to arrest the tyrannical hands of the ministry and Parliament. Our petitions have been slighted; our remonstrances have produced additional violence and insult; our supplications have been disregarded; and we have been spurned, with contempt, from the foot of the throne! In vain, after these things, may we indulge the fond hope of peace and reconciliation. There is no longer any room for hope. If we wish to be free—if we mean to preserve inviolate those inestimable privileges for which we have been so long contending—if we mean not basely to abandon the noble struggle in which we have been so long engaged, and which we have pledged ourselves never to abandon until the glorious object of our contest shall be obtained—we must fight! I repeat it, sir, we must fight! An appeal to arms and to the God of hosts is all that is left us!

They tell us, Sir, that we are weak; unable to cope with so formidable an adversary. But when shall we be stronger? Will it be the next week, or the next year? Will it be when we are totally disarmed, and when a British guard shall be stationed in every house? Shall we gather strength by irresolution and inaction? Shall we acquire the means of effectual resistance by lying supinely on our backs and hugging the delusive phantom of hope, until our enemies shall have bound us hand and foot? Sir, we are not weak if we make a proper use of those means which the God of nature hath placed in our power. The millions of people, armed in the holy cause of liberty, and in such a country as that which we possess, are invincible by any force which our enemy can send against us. Besides, sir, we shall not fight our battles alone. There is a just God who presides over the destinies of nations, and who will raise up friends to fight our battles for us. The battle, sir, is not to the strong alone; it is to the vigilant, the active, the brave. Besides, sir, we have no election. If we were base enough to desire it, it is now too late to retire from the contest. There is no retreat but in submission and slavery! Our chains are forged! Their clanking may be heard on the plains of Boston! The war is inevitable—and let it come! I repeat it, Sir, let it come.

It is in vain, sir, to extenuate the matter. Gentlemen may cry, Peace, Peace—but there is no peace. The war is actually begun! The next gale that sweeps from the north will bring to our ears the clash of resounding arms! Our brethren are already in the field! Why stand we here idle? What is it that gentlemen wish? What would they have? Is life so dear, or peace so sweet, as to be purchased at the price of chains and slavery? Forbid it, Almighty God! I know not what course others may take; but as for me, give me liberty or give me death!

Our brethren are already in the field! Why stand we here idle? What is it that gentlemen wish? What would they have? Is life so dear, or peace so sweet, as to be purchased at the price of chains and slavery? Forbid it, Almighty God! I know not what course others may take; but as for me, give me liberty or give me death!

Model Practice 1

Model Practice 2

Model Practice 3

Common Sense (excerpt)
by Thomas Paine
February 14, 1776

Introduction

Perhaps the sentiments contained in the following pages, are not yet sufficiently fashionable to procure them general favor; a long habit of not thinking a thing wrong gives it a superficial appearance of being right and raises at first a formidable outcry in defense of custom. But tumult soon subsides. Time makes more converts than reason.

As a long and violent abuse of power is generally the means of calling the right of it in question, (and in matters too which might never have been thought of, had not the sufferers been aggravated into the inquiry,) and as the king of England hath undertaken in his own right, to support the parliament in what he calls theirs, and as the good people of this country are grievously oppressed by the combination, they have an undoubted privilege to inquire into the pretensions of both, and equally to reject the usurpations of either.

In the following sheets, the author hath studiously avoided every thing which is personal among ourselves. Compliments as well as censure to individuals make no part thereof. The wise and the worthy need not the triumph of a pamphlet; and those whose sentiments are injudicious or unfriendly, will cease of themselves, unless too much pains is bestowed upon their conversion.

The cause of America is, in a great measure, the cause of all mankind. Many circumstances have, and will arise, which are not local, but universal, and through which the principles of all lovers of mankind are affected, and in the event of which, their affections are interested. The laying a country desolate with fire and sword, declaring war against the natural rights of all mankind, and extirpating the defenders thereof from the face of the earth, is the concern of every man to whom nature hath given the power of feeling; of which class, regardless of party censure, is

The author.
Philadelphia, Feb. 14, 1776.

Of the Present Ability of America, with some miscellaneous Reflections

The infant state of the Colonies, as it is called, so far from being against, is an argument in favour of independence. We are sufficiently numerous, and were we more so, we might be less united. It is a matter worthy of observation, that the more a country is peopled, the smaller their armies are. In military numbers, the ancients far exceeded the moderns: and the reason is evident. For trade being the consequence of population, men become too much absorbed thereby to attend to anything else. Commerce diminishes the spirit, both of patriotism and military defense. And history sufficiently informs us, that the bravest achievements were always accomplished in the non-age of a nation. With the increase of commerce, England hath lost its spirit. The city of London, notwithstanding its numbers, submits to continued insults with the patience of a coward. The more men have to lose, the less willing are they to venture. The rich are in general slaves to fear, and submit to courtly power with the trembling duplicity of a Spaniel.

Appendix

However, it matters very little now, what the king of England either says or does; he hath wickedly broken through every moral and human obligation, trampled nature and conscience beneath his feet; and by a steady and constitutional spirit of insolence and cruelty, procured for himself an universal hatred. It is NOW the interest of America to provide for herself. She hath already a large and young family, whom it is more her duty to take care of, than to be granting away her property, to support a power who is become a reproach to the names of men and Christians—YE, whose office it is to watch over the morals of a nation, of whatsoever sect or denomination ye are of, as well as ye, who, are more immediately the guardians of the public liberty, if ye wish to preserve your native country uncontaminated by European corruption, ye must in secret wish a separation.

With the increase of commerce, England hath lost its spirit. The city of London, notwithstanding its numbers, submits to continued insults with the patience of a coward. The more men have to lose, the less willing are they to venture. The rich are in general slaves to fear, and submit to courtly power with the trembling duplicity of a Spaniel.

Model Practice 1

Model Practice 2

Model Practice 3

The Declaration of Independence of The United States of America

In Congress, July 4, 1776

The unanimous Declaration of the thirteen united States of America

When in the Course of human events, it becomes necessary for one people to dissolve the political bands which have connected them with another, and to assume, among the Powers of the earth, the separate and equal station to which the Laws of Nature and of Nature's God entitle them, a decent respect to the opinions of mankind requires that they should declare the causes which impel them to the separation.

We hold these truths to be self-evident, that all men are created equal, that they are endowed by their Creator with certain unalienable Rights, that among these are Life, Liberty, and the pursuit of Happiness.—That to secure these rights, Governments are instituted among Men, deriving their just powers from the consent of the governed,—That whenever any Form of Government becomes destructive of these ends, it is the Right of the People to alter or to abolish it, and to institute new Government, laying its foundation on such principles and organizing its powers in such form, as to them shall seem most likely to effect their Safety and Happiness. Prudence, indeed, will dictate that Governments long established should not be changed for light and transient causes; and accordingly all experience hath shown, that mankind are more disposed to suffer, while evils are sufferable, than to right themselves by abolishing the forms to which they are accustomed. But when a long train of abuses and usurpations, pursuing invariably the same Object evinces a design to reduce them under absolute Despotism, it is their right, it is their duty, to throw off such Government, and to provide new Guards for their future security.—Such has been the patient sufferance of these Colonies; and such is now the necessity which constrains them to alter their former Systems of Government. The history of the present King of Great Britain is a history of repeated injuries and usurpations, all having in direct object the establishment of an absolute Tyranny over these States. To prove this, let Facts be submitted to a candid world.

> He has refused his Assent to Laws, the most wholesome and necessary for the public good.
> He has forbidden his Governors to pass Laws of immediate and pressing importance, unless suspended in their operation till his Assent should be obtained; and when so suspended, he has utterly neglected to attend to them.
> He has refused to pass other Laws for the accommodation of large districts of people, unless those people would relinquish the right of Representation in the Legislature, a right inestimable to them and formidable to tyrants only.
> He has called together legislative bodies at places unusual, uncomfortable, and distant from the depository of their Public Records, for the sole purpose of fatiguing them into compliance with his measures.
> He has dissolved Representative Houses repeatedly, for opposing with manly firmness his invasions on the rights of the people.
> He has refused for a long time, after such dissolutions, to cause others to be elected; whereby the Legislative Powers, incapable of Annihilation, have returned to the People at large for their exercise; the State remaining in the mean time exposed to all the dangers of invasion from without, and convulsions within.
> He has endeavoured to prevent the population of these States; for that purpose obstructing the Laws of Naturalization of Foreigners; refusing to pass others to encourage their migration hither, and raising the conditions of new Appropriations of Lands.

He has obstructed the Administration of Justice, by refusing his Assent to Laws for establishing Judiciary Powers.

He has made judges dependent on his Will alone, for the tenure of their offices, and the amount and payment of their salaries.

He has erected a multitude of New Offices, and sent hither swarms of Officers to harass our People, and eat out their substance.

He has kept among us, in times of peace, Standing Armies without the Consent of our legislatures.

He has affected to render the Military independent of and superior to the Civil Power.

He has combined with others to subject us to a jurisdiction foreign to our constitution, and unacknowledged by our laws; giving his Assent to their Acts of pretended legislation:

For quartering large bodies of armed troops among us:

For protecting them, by a mock Trial, from Punishment for any Murders which they should commit on the Inhabitants of these States:

For cutting off our Trade with all parts of the world:

For imposing taxes on us without our Consent:

For depriving us, in many cases, of the benefits of Trial by Jury:

For transporting us beyond Seas to be tried for pretended offences:

For abolishing the free System of English Laws in a neighbouring Province, establishing therein an Arbitrary government, and enlarging its Boundaries so as to render it at once an example and fit instrument for introducing the same absolute rule into these Colonies:

For taking away our Charters, abolishing our most valuable Laws, and altering fundamentally the Forms of our Governments:

For suspending our own Legislatures, and declaring themselves invested with Power to legislate for us in all cases whatsoever.

He has abdicated Government here, by declaring us out of his Protection and waging War against us.

He has plundered our seas, ravaged our Coasts, burnt our towns, and destroyed the lives of our people.

He is at this time transporting large armies of foreign mercenaries to complete the works of death, desolation and tyranny, already begun with circumstances of Cruelty & perfidy scarcely paralleled in the most barbarous ages, and totally unworthy of the Head of a civilized nation.

He has constrained our fellow Citizens taken Captive on the high Seas to bear Arms against their Country, to become the executioners of their friends and Brethren, or to fall themselves by their Hands.

He has excited domestic insurrections amongst us, and has endeavoured to bring on the inhabitants of our frontiers, the merciless Indian Savages, whose known rule of warfare, is an undistinguished destruction of all ages, sexes and conditions.

In every stage of these Oppressions We have Petitioned for Redress in the most humble terms: Our repeated Petitions have been answered only by repeated injury. A Prince, whose character is thus marked by every act which may define a Tyrant, is unfit to be the ruler of a free People.

Nor have We been wanting in attention to our British brethren. We have warned them from time to time of attempts by their legislature to extend an unwarrantable jurisdiction over us. We have reminded them of the circumstances of our emigration and settlement here. We have appealed to their native justice and magnanimity, and we have conjured them by the ties of our common kindred to disavow these usurpations, which would inevitably interrupt our connections and correspondence.

They too have been deaf to the voice of justice and of consanguinity. We must, therefore, acquiesce in the necessity, which denounces our Separation, and hold them, as we hold the rest of mankind, Enemies in War, in Peace Friends.

We, therefore, the Representatives of the United States of America, in General Congress, Assembled, appealing to the Supreme Judge of the world for the rectitude of our intentions, do, in the Name, and by the Authority of the good People of these Colonies, solemnly publish and declare, That these United Colonies are, and of Right ought to be Free and Independent States; that they are Absolved from all Allegiance to the British Crown, and that all political connection between them and the State of Great Britain, is and ought to be totally dissolved; and that as Free and Independent States, they have full Power to levy War, conclude Peace, contract Alliances, establish Commerce, and to do all other Acts and Things which Independent States may of right do. And for the support of this Declaration, with a firm reliance on the Protection of Divine Providence, we mutually pledge to each other our Lives, our Fortunes and our sacred Honor.

Button Gwinnett	Lyman Hall	George Walton
William Hooper	Joseph Hewes	John Penn
Edward Rutledge	Thomas Heyward, Jr	Thomas Lunch, Jr.
Arthur Middleton	John Hancock	Samuel Chase
William Paca	Thomas Stone	Charles Carroll of Carrollton
George Wythe	Richard Henry Lee	Thomas Jefferson
Benjamin Harrison	Thomas Nelson, Jr.	Francis Lightfoot Lee
Carter Braxton	Robert Morris	Benjamin Rush
Benjamin Franklin	John Morton	George Clymer
James Smith	George Taylor	James Wilson
George Ross	Caesar Rodney	George Read
Thomas McKean	William Floyd	Philip Livingston
Francis Lewis	Lewis Morris	Richard Stockton
John Witherspoon	Francis Hopkinson	John Hart
Abraham Clark	Josiah Bartlett	William Whipple
Samuel Adams	John Adams	Robert Treat Paine
Elbridge Gerry	Stephen Hopkins	William Ellery
Roger Sherman	Samuel Huntington	William Williams
Oliver Wolcott	Matthew Thornton	

When in the Course of human events, it becomes necessary for one people to dissolve the political bands which have connected them with another, and to assume, among the Powers of the earth, the separate and equal station to which the Laws of Nature and of Nature's God entitle them, a decent respect to the opinions of mankind requires that they should declare the causes which impel them to the separation.

Model Practice 1

Model Practice 2

Model Practice 3

Preamble to The Constitution of The United States of America 1787

We the people of the United States, in Order to form a more perfect Union, establish Justice, insure domestic Tranquility, provide for the common defense, promote the general Welfare, and secure the Blessings of Liberty to ourselves and our Posterity, do ordain and establish this Constitution for the United States of America.

Elements from
The Constitution of The United States of America

John L. Hülshof

1. Congress must meet at least once a year.(Congress consists of the Senate and the House of Representatives.)

2. One State cannot undo the acts of another.

3. Congress may admit any number of new States.

4. One State must respect the laws and legal decisions of another.

5. Every citizen is guaranteed a speedy trial by jury.

6. Congress cannot pass a law to punish a crime already committed.

7. Bills of revenue can originate only in the House of Representatives.

8. A person committing a crime in one State cannot find refuge in another.

9. The Constitution forbids excessive bail or cruel punishment.

10. Treaties with foreign countries are made by the President and ratified by the Senate.

11. Writing alone does not constitute treason against the United States. There must be an overt act.

12. An Act of Congress cannot become law over the vote of the President except by a two-thirds vote of both Houses.

13. Only a natural-born citizen of the United States can become President or Vice-President of the United States.

We the people of the United States, in Order to form a more perfect Union, establish Justice, insure domestic Tranquility, provide for the common defense, promote the general Welfare, and secure the Blessings of Liberty to ourselves and our Posterity, do ordain and establish this Constitution for the United States of America.

Model Practice 1

Model Practice 2

Model Practice 3

To James Madison (excerpt)

Paris, December 20, 1787

Dear Sir,

I like much the general idea of framing a government which should go on of itself, peaceably, without needing continual recurrence to the State legislatures. I like the organization of the government into legislative, judiciary, and executive. I like the power given the legislature to levy taxes, and for that reason solely, I approve of the greater House being chosen by the people directly. For though I think a House, so chosen, will be very far inferior to the present Congress, will be very illy qualified to legislate for the Union, for foreign nations, &c.; yet this evil does not weigh against the good of preserving inviolate the fundamental principle, that the people are not to be taxed but by representatives chosen immediately by themselves. I am captivated by the compromise of the opposite claims of the great and little States, of the latter to equal, and the former to proportional influence. I am much pleased, too, with the substitution of the method of voting by persons, instead of that of voting by States: and I like the negative given to the Executive, conjointly with a third of either House; though I should have liked it better, had the judiciary been associated for that purpose, or invested separately with a similar power. There are other good things of less moment.

I will now tell you what I do not like. First, the omission of a bill of rights, providing clearly, and without the aid of sophism, for freedom of religion, freedom of the press, protection against standing armies, restriction of monopolies, the eternal and unremitting force of the habeas corpus laws, and trials by jury in all matters of fact triable by the laws of the land, and not by the laws of nations. To say, as Mr. Wilson does, that a bill of rights was not necessary, because all is reserved in the case of the general government which is not given, while in the particular ones, all is given which is not reserved, might do for the audience to which it was addressed: but it is surely a gratis dictum, the reverse of which might just as well be said; and it is opposed by strong inferences from the body of the instrument, as well as from the omission of the clause of our present Confederation, which had made the reservation in express terms. It was hard to conclude, because there has been a want of uniformity among the States as to the cases triable by jury, because some have been so incautious as to dispense with this mode of trial in certain cases, therefore the more prudent States shall be reduced to the same level of calamity. It would have been much more just and wise to have concluded the other way, that as most of the States had preserved with jealousy this sacred palladium of liberty, those who had wandered, should be brought back to it: and to have established general right rather than general wrong. For I consider all the ill as established, which maybe established. I have a right to nothing, which another has a right to take away; and Congress will have a right to take away trials by jury in all civil cases. Let me add, that a bill of rights is what the people are entitled to against every government on earth, general or particular; and what no just government should refuse, or rest on inference.

The second feature I dislike, and strongly dislike, is the abandonment, in every instance, of the principle of rotation in office, and most particularly in the case of the President. Reason and experience tell us, that the first magistrate will always be re-elected if he may be re-elected. He is then an officer for life.

Th: Jefferson.

I will now tell you what I do not like. First, the omission of a bill of rights, providing clearly, and without the aid of sophism, for freedom of religion, freedom of the press, protection against standing armies, restriction of monopolies, the eternal and unremitting force of the habeas corpus laws, and trials by jury in all matters of fact triable by the laws of the land, and not by the laws of nations.

Model Practice 1

Model Practice 2

Model Practice 3

The United States Bill of Rights

The Ten Original Amendments to the Constitution of the United States
Passed by Congress September 25, 1789
Ratified December 15, 1791

I
Congress shall make no law respecting an establishment of religion, or prohibiting the free exercise thereof; or abridging the freedom of speech, or of the press, or the right of the people peaceably to assemble, and to petition the Government for a redress of grievances.

II
A well-regulated militia, being necessary to the security of a free State, the right of the people to keep and bear arms, shall not be infringed.

III
No soldier shall, in time of peace be quartered in any house, without the consent of the owner, nor in time of war, but in a manner to be prescribed by law.

IV
The right of the people to be secure in their persons, houses, papers, and effects, against unreasonable searches and seizures, shall not be violated, and no Warrants shall issue, but upon probable cause, supported by oath or affirmation, and particularly describing the place to be searched, and the persons or things to be seized.

V
No person shall be held to answer for a capital, or otherwise infamous crime, unless on a presentment or indictment of a Grand Jury, except in cases arising in the land or naval forces, or in the Militia, when in actual service in time of War or public danger; nor shall any person be subject for the same offense to be twice put in jeopardy of life or limb; nor shall be compelled in any criminal case to be a witness against himself, nor be deprived of life, liberty, or property, without due process of law; nor shall private property be taken for public use without just compensation.

VI
In all criminal prosecutions, the accused shall enjoy the right to a speedy and public trial, by an impartial jury of the State and district wherein the crime shall have been committed, which district shall have been previously ascertained by law, and to be informed of the nature and cause of the accusation; to be confronted with the witnesses against him; to have compulsory process for obtaining witnesses in his favor, and to have the assistance of counsel for his defense.

VII
In suits at common law, where the value in controversy shall exceed twenty dollars, the right of trial by jury shall be preserved, and no fact tried by a jury shall be otherwise re-examined in any court of the United States, than according to the rules of the common law.

VIII
Excessive bail shall not be required nor excessive fines imposed, nor cruel and unusual punishments inflicted.

IX

The enumeration in the Constitution, of certain rights, shall not be construed to deny or disparage others retained by the people.

X

The powers not delegated to the United States by the Constitution, nor prohibited by it to the States, are reserved to the States respectively, or to the people.

I. Congress shall make no law respecting an establishment of religion, or prohibiting the free exercise thereof; or abridging the freedom of speech, or of the press, or the right of the people peaceably to assemble, and to petition the Government for a redress of grievances.

Model Practice 1

Model Practice 2

Model Practice 3

Proclamation
A National Thanksgiving

Whereas it is the duty of all nations to acknowledge the providence of Almighty God, to obey His will, to be grateful for His benefits, and humbly to implore His protection and favor; and

Whereas both Houses of Congress have, by their joint committee, requested me "to recommend to the people of the United States a day of public thanksgiving and prayer, to be observed by acknowledging with grateful hearts the many and signal favors of Almighty God, especially by affording them an opportunity peaceably to establish a form of government for their safety and happiness:"

Now, therefore, I do recommend and assign Thursday, the 26th day of November next, to be devoted by the people of these States to the service of that great and glorious Being who is the beneficent author of all the good that was, that is, or that will be; that we may then all unite in rendering unto Him our sincere and humble thanks for His kind care and protection of the people of this country previous to their becoming a nation; for the signal and manifold mercies and the favorable interpositions of His providence in the course and conclusion of the late war; for the great degree of tranquillity, union, and plenty which we have since enjoyed; for the peaceable and rational manner in which we have been enabled to establish constitutions of government for our safety and happiness, and particularly the national one now lately instituted; for the civil and religious liberty with which we are blessed, and the means we have of acquiring and diffusing useful knowledge; and, in general, for all the great and various favors which He has been pleased to confer upon us.

And also that we may then unite in most humbly offering our prayers and supplications to the great Lord and Ruler of Nations and beseech Him to pardon our national and other transgressions; to enable us all, whether in public or private stations, to perform our several and relative duties properly and punctually; to render our National Government a blessing to all the people by constantly being a Government of wise, just, and constitutional laws, discreetly and faithfully executed and obeyed; to protect and guide all sovereigns and nations (especially such as have shown kindness to us), and to bless them with good governments, peace, and concord; to promote the knowledge and practice of true religion and virtue, and the increase of science among them and us; and, generally, to grant unto all mankind such a degree of temporal prosperity as He alone knows to be best.

Given under my hand, at the city of New York, the 3d day of October, A.D. 1789.

GEORGE WASHINGTON.

Now, therefore, I do recommend and assign Thursday, the 26th day of November next, to be devoted by the people of these States to the service of that great and glorious Being who is the beneficent author of all the good that was, that is, or that will be; that we may then all unite in rendering unto Him our sincere and humble thanks for His kind care and protection of the people of this country previous to their becoming a nation.

Model Practice 1

Model Practice 2

Model Practice 3

George Washington's Farewell Address (excerpt)

UNITED STATES, September 17, 1796.

Friends and Fellow-Citizens:

The period for a new election of a citizen to administer the Executive Government of the United States being not far distant, and the time actually arrived when your thoughts must be employed in designating the person who is to be clothed with that important trust, it appears to me proper, especially as it may conduce to a more distinct expression of the public voice, that I should now apprise you of the resolution I have formed to decline being considered among the number of those out of whom a choice is to be made.

I beg you at the same time to do me the justice to be assured that this resolution has not been taken without a strict regard to all the considerations appertaining to the relation which binds a dutiful citizen to his country; and that in withdrawing the tender of service, which silence in my situation might imply, I am influenced by no diminution of zeal for your future interest, no deficiency of grateful respect for your past kindness, but am supported by a full conviction that the step is compatible with both.

Though in reviewing the incidents of my Administration I am unconscious of intentional error; I am, nevertheless, too sensible of my defects not to think it probable that I may have committed many errors. Whatever they may be, I fervently beseech the Almighty to avert or mitigate the evils to which they may tend. I shall also carry with me the hope that my country will never cease to view them with indulgence, and that, after forty-five years of my life dedicated to its service with an upright zeal, the faults of incompetent abilities will be consigned to oblivion, as myself must soon be to the mansions of rest.

Relying on its kindness in this as in other things, and actuated by that fervent love toward it which is so natural to a man who views in it the native soil of himself and his progenitors for several generations, I anticipate with pleasing expectation that retreat in which I promise myself to realize without alloy the sweet enjoyment of partaking in the midst of my fellow-citizens the benign influence of good laws under a free government—the ever-favorite object of my heart, and the happy reward, as I trust, of our mutual cares, labors, and dangers.

GEORGE WASHINGTON.

The period for a new election of a citizen to administer the Executive Government of the United States being not far distant, and the time actually arrived when your thoughts must be employed in designating the person who is to be clothed with that important trust, it appears to me proper, especially as it may conduce to a more distinct expression of the public voice, that I should now apprise you of the resolution I have formed to decline being considered among the number of those out of whom a choice is to be made.

Model Practice 1

Model Practice 2

Model Practice 3

Jefferson's Letter to the Danbury Baptists

To messers. Nehemiah Dodge, Ephraim Robbins, & Stephen S. Nelson, a committee of the Danbury Baptist association in the state of Connecticut.

Gentlemen

The affectionate sentiments of esteem and approbation which you are so good as to express towards me, on behalf of the Danbury Baptist association, give me the highest satisfaction. My duties dictate a faithful and zealous pursuit of the interests of my constituents, and in proportion as they are persuaded of my fidelity to those duties, the discharge of them becomes more and more pleasing.

Believing with you that religion is a matter which lies solely between Man and his God, that he owes account to none other for his faith or his worship, that the legitimate powers of government reach actions only, & not opinions, I contemplate with sovereign reverence that act of the whole American people which declared that their legislature should "make no law respecting an establishment of religion, or prohibiting the free exercise thereof," thus building a wall of separation between Church & State. Adhering to this expression of the supreme will of the nation in behalf of the rights of conscience, I shall see with sincere satisfaction the progress of those sentiments which tend to restore to man all his natural rights, convinced he has no natural right in opposition to his social duties.

I reciprocate your kind prayers for the protection & blessing of the common father and creator of man, and tender you for yourselves & your religious association, assurances of my high respect & esteem.

Th Jefferson
Jan. 1. 1802.

Believing with you that religion is a matter which lies solely between Man and his God, that he owes account to none other for his faith or his worship, that the legitimate powers of government reach actions only and not opinions, I contemplate with sovereign reverence that act of the whole American people which declared that their legislature should "make no law respecting an establishment of religion, or prohibiting the free exercise thereof," thus building a wall of separation between Church and State.

Model Practice 1

Model Practice 2

Model Practice 3

Transcript of President Andrew Jackson's Message to Congress 'On Indian Removal' (1830)

Andrew Jackson's Annual Message

It gives me pleasure to announce to Congress that the benevolent policy of the Government, steadily pursued for nearly thirty years, in relation to the removal of the Indians beyond the white settlements is approaching to a happy consummation. Two important tribes have accepted the provision made for their removal at the last session of Congress, and it is believed that their example will induce the remaining tribes also to seek the same obvious advantages.

The consequences of a speedy removal will be important to the United States, to individual States, and to the Indians themselves. The pecuniary advantages which it promises to the Government are the least of its recommendations. It puts an end to all possible danger of collision between the authorities of the General and State Governments on account of the Indians. It will place a dense and civilized population in large tracts of country now occupied by a few savage hunters. By opening the whole territory between Tennessee on the north and Louisiana on the south to the settlement of the whites it will incalculably strengthen the southwestern frontier and render the adjacent States strong enough to repel future invasions without remote aid. It will relieve the whole State of Mississippi and the western part of Alabama of Indian occupancy, and enable those States to advance rapidly in population, wealth, and power. It will separate the Indians from immediate contact with settlements of whites; free them from the power of the States; enable them to pursue happiness in their own way and under their own rude institutions; will retard the progress of decay, which is lessening their numbers, and perhaps cause them gradually, under the protection of the Government and through the influence of good counsels, to cast off their savage habits and become an interesting, civilized, and Christian community.

What good man would prefer a country covered with forests and ranged by a few thousand savages to our extensive Republic, studded with cities, towns, and prosperous farms embellished with all the improvements which art can devise or industry execute, occupied by more than 12,000,000 happy people, and filled with all the blessings of liberty, civilization and religion?

The present policy of the Government is but a continuation of the same progressive change by a milder process. The tribes which occupied the countries now constituting the Eastern States were annihilated or have melted away to make room for the whites. The waves of population and civilization are rolling to the westward, and we now propose to acquire the countries occupied by the red men of the South and West by a fair exchange, and at the expense of the United States, to send them to land where their existence may be prolonged and perhaps made perpetual. Doubtless it will be painful to leave the graves of their fathers; but what do they more than our ancestors did or than our children are now doing? To better their condition in an unknown land our forefathers left all that was dear in earthly objects. Our children by thousands yearly leave the land of their birth to seek new homes in distant regions. Does Humanity weep at these painful separations from everything, animate and inanimate, with which the young heart has become entwined? Far from it. It is rather a source of joy that our country affords scope where our young population may range unconstrained in body or in mind, developing the power and facilities of man in their highest perfection. These remove hundreds and almost thousands of miles at their own expense, purchase the lands they occupy, and support themselves at their new homes from the moment of their arrival. Can it be cruel in this Government when, by events which it can not control, the Indian is made discontented in his ancient home to purchase his lands, to give him a new and extensive territory, to pay the expense of his removal, and support him a year in his new abode? How many thousands of our own people would gladly embrace the opportunity of removing to the West on such conditions! If the offers made to the Indians were extended to them, they would be hailed with gratitude and joy.

And is it supposed that the wandering savage has a stronger attachment to his home than the settled, civilized Christian? Is it more afflicting to him to leave the graves of his fathers than it is to our brothers and children? Rightly considered, the policy of the General Government toward the red man is not only liberal, but generous. He is unwilling to submit to the laws of the States and mingle with their population. To save him from this alternative, or perhaps utter annihilation, the General Government kindly offers him a new home, and proposes to pay the whole expense of his removal and settlement.

Rightly considered, the policy of the General Government toward the red man is not only liberal, but generous. He is unwilling to submit to the laws of the States and mingle with their population. To save him from this alternative, or perhaps utter annihilation, the General Government kindly offers him a new home, and proposes to pay the whole expense of his removal and settlement.

Model Practice 1

Model Practice 2

Model Practice 3

Life of Tecumseh, and of His Brother The Prophet (excerpt Ch.16, pg. 224 and 225)
With a Historical Sketch of the Shawanoe Indians
by Benjamin Drake
Published 1841

TECUMSEH was near six feet in stature with a compact, muscular frame, capable of great physical endurance. His head was of a moderate size, with a forehead full and high; his nose slightly aquiline, teeth large and regular, eyes black, penetrating and overhung with heavy arched brows, which increased the uniformly grave and severe expression of his countenance. He is represented, by those who knew him, to have been a remarkably fine looking man, always plain but neat in his dress, and of a commanding personal presence. His portrait, it is believed, was never painted, owing probably to his strong prejudices against the whites.

From his boyhood, Tecumseh was remarkable for temperance and the strictest integrity. He was hospitable, generous and humane; and these traits were acknowledged in his character long before he rose to distinction, or had conceived the project of that union of the tribes, on which the energies of his manhood were fruitlessly expended. He was, says an intelligent Shawanoe, who had known him from childhood, kind and attentive to the aged and infirm, looking personally to their comfort, repairing their frail wigwams when winter approached, giving them skins for moccasins and clothing, and sharing with them the choicest game which the woods and the seasons afforded. Nor were these acts of kindness bestowed exclusively on those of rank or reputation. On the contrary, he made it his business to search out the humblest objects of charity, and in a quick, unostentatious manner, relieve their wants.

The moral and intellectual qualities of Tecumseh place him above the age and the race in which his lot was cast. "From the earliest period of his life," says Mr. Johnston, the late Indian agent at Piqua, "Tecumseh was distinguished for virtue, for a strict adherence to truth, honor, and integrity. He was sober and abstemious, never indulging in the use of liquor nor eating to excess." Another respectable individual, who resided for near twenty years as a prisoner among the Shawanoes, and part of that time in the family of Tecumseh, writes to us, "I know of no peculiarity about him that gained him popularity. His talents, rectitude of deportment, and friendly disposition, commanded the respect and regard of all about him. In short, I consider him a very great as well as a very good man, who, had he enjoyed the advantages of a liberal education, would have done honor to any age or any nation."

He was, says an intelligent Shawanoe, who had known him from childhood, kind and attentive to the aged and infirm, looking personally to their comfort, repairing their frail wigwams when winter approached, giving them skins for moccasins and clothing, and sharing with them the choicest game which the woods and the seasons afforded. Nor were these acts of kindness bestowed exclusively on those of rank or reputation.

Model Practice 1

Model Practice 2

Model Practice 3

Life and Adventures of Black Hawk (excerpt, chapter 9)

Entered according to Act of Congress, in the year 1843,
By George Conclin,
In the Clerk's Office of the District of Ohio.

For the particulars, given below, of the last days and death of Black Hawk, we are indebted to a highly respectable gentleman, W. Henry Starr, Esq. of Burlington, Iowa Territory.

Your letter of the 2nd of January came to hand in due course of mail, in which you make some enquiries concerning the old chief of the Sac and Fox tribes—the venerable Black Hawk. I should have replied to it sooner, could I have done so satisfactorily either to you or myself. I knew much by report of the old chief, and something from personal acquaintance; but my knowledge was not so accurate as to be serviceable to a faithful biographer. I have, therefore, taken sometime to make the necessary enquiries, and satisfy myself of their accuracy.

After Black Hawk's last return from the eastern states, he passed the winter of 1837-8 in the county of Lee, in the southeastern portion of this territory, on a small stream called Devil-creek. The white settlements extended for forty miles west of him, and the tribe to which he belonged, with the exception of a few old braves, and his family, resided on the frontier. From his tribe he was isolated in position and feeling. His family consisted of a wife, two sons, Nasheaskuk and Samesett, (as they are pronounced here,) a daughter and her husband. They passed their time principally in hunting deer, wild turkeys, and the prairie hen, which are abundant in that quarter of the territory. For hunting, Black Hawk is said to have displayed no fondness; but chose to spend his time in improving his place of residence, and exercising his ingenuity with mechanic tools. In the spring of 1838, they removed to the frontier, and settled upon the Des Moines river, about eighty or ninety miles from its mouth, near to a trading post, and in the immediate vicinity of the villages of the other chiefs of the tribe. Here he had a very comfortable bark cabin, which he furnished in imitation of the whites, with chairs, a table, a mirror, and mattresses. His dress was that of the other chiefs, with the exception of a broad-brimmed black hat, which he usually wore. In the summer he cultivated a few acres of land in corn, melons, and various kinds of vegetables. He was frequently visited by the whites, and I have often heard his hospitality highly commended.

On the 4th of July last, he was present at Fort Madison, in Lee county, by special invitation, and was the most conspicuous guest of the citizens assembled in commemoration of that day. Among the toasts called forth by the occasion was the following:

"Our illustrious guest, Black Hawk. May his declining years be as calm and serene as his previous life has been boisterous and full of warlike incidents. His attachment and present friendship to his white brethren fully entitle him to a seat at our festive board."

So soon as this sentiment was drank, Black Hawk arose and delivered the following speech, which was taken down at the time by two interpreters, and by them furnished for publication:

"It has pleased the Great Spirit that I am here today. I have eaten with my white friends. The earth is our mother. We are now on it, with the Great Spirit above us. It is good. I hope we are all friends here. A few winters ago, I was fighting against you. I did wrong, perhaps; but that is past. It is buried. Let it be forgotten.

"Rock river was a beautiful country. I liked my towns, my cornfields, and the home of my people. I fought for it. It is now yours. Keep it as we did. It will produce you good crops.

"I thank the Great Spirit that I am now friendly with my white brethren. We are here together. We have eaten together. We are friends. It is his wish and mine. I thank you for your friendship."

Here he had a very comfortable bark cabin, which he furnished in imitation of the whites, with chairs, a table, a mirror, and mattresses. His dress was that of the other chiefs, with the exception of a broad-brimmed black hat, which he usually wore. In the summer he cultivated a few acres of land in corn, melons, and various kinds of vegetables. He was frequently visited by the whites, and I have often heard his hospitality highly commended.

Model Practice 1

Model Practice 2

Model Practice 3

Narrative of the Life and Adventures of Henry Bibb, (excerpt, page 15)
An American Slave, written by Himself
Published 1849

I was born May 1815, of a slave mother, in Shelby County, Kentucky, and was claimed as the property of David White Esq. He came into possession of my mother long before I was born. I was brought up in the Counties of Shelby, Henry, Oldham, and Trimble. Or more correctly speaking, in the above counties, I may safely say, I was flogged up; for where I should have received moral, mental, and religious instruction, I received stripes without number, the object of which was to degrade and keep me in subordination. I can truly say that I drank deeply of the bitter cup of suffering and woe. I have been dragged down to the lowest depths of human degradation and wretchedness by Slaveholders.

The first time I was separated from my mother, Mildred Jackson, I was young and small. I knew nothing of my condition then as a slave. I was living with Mr. White, whose wife died and left him a widower with one little girl, who was said to be the legitimate owner of my mother, and all her children. This girl was also my playmate when we were children.

I was taken away from my mother, and hired out to labor for various persons, eight or ten years in succession; and all my wages were expended for the education of Harriet White, my playmate. It was then my sorrows and sufferings commenced. It was then I first commenced seeing and feeling that I was a wretched slave, compelled to work under the lash without wages, and often without clothes enough to hide my nakedness. I have often worked without half enough to eat, both late and early, by day and by night. I have often laid my wearied limbs down at night to rest upon a dirt floor, or a bench, without any covering at all, because I had no where else to rest my wearied body, after having worked hard all the day. I have also been compelled in early life, to go at the bidding of a tyrant, through all kinds of weather, hot or cold, wet or dry, and without shoes frequently, until the month of December, with my bare feet on the cold frosty ground, cracked open and bleeding as I walked. Reader, believe me when I say, that no tongue, nor pen ever has or can express the horrors of American Slavery. Consequently I despair in finding language to express adequately the deep feeling of my soul, as I contemplate the past history of my life. But although I have suffered much from the lash, and for want of food and raiment; I confess that it was no disadvantage to be passed through the hands of so many families, as the only source of information that I had to enlighten my mind, consisted in what I could see and hear from others. Slaves were not allowed books, pen, ink, nor paper, to improve their minds. But it seems to me now, that I was particularly observing, and apt to retain what came under my observation. But more especially, all that I heard about liberty and freedom to the slaves, I never forgot. Among other good trades I learned the art of running away to perfection. I made a regular business of it, and never gave it up, until I had broken the bands of slavery, and landed myself safely in Canada, where I was regarded as a man, and not as a thing.

Or more correctly speaking, in the above counties, I may safely say, I was flogged up; for where I should have received moral, mental, and religious instruction, I received stripes without number, the object of which was to degrade and keep me in subordination. I can truly say that I drank deeply of the bitter cup of suffering and woe. I have been dragged down to the lowest depths of human degradation and wretchedness by Slaveholders.

Model Practice 1

Model Practice 2

Model Practice 3

On the Duty of Civil Disobedience (excerpt)
by Henry David Thoreau
Published 1849
Original title: Resistance to Civil Government

I heartily accept the motto "That government is best which governs least"; and I should like to see it acted up to more rapidly and systematically. Carried out, it finally amounts to this, which also I believe—"That government is best which governs not at all"; and when men are prepared for it, that will be the kind of government which they will have. Government is at best but an expedient; but most governments are usually, and all governments are sometimes, inexpedient. The objections which have been brought against a standing army, and they are many and weighty and deserve to prevail, may also at last be brought against a standing government. The standing army is only an arm of the standing government. The government itself, which is only the mode which the people have chosen to execute their will, is equally liable to be abused and perverted before the people can act through it. Witness the present Mexican war, the work of comparatively a few individuals using the standing government as their tool; for in the outset, the people would not have consented to this measure.

He who gives himself entirely to his fellow men appears to them useless and selfish; but he who gives himself partially to them is pronounced a benefactor and philanthropist.

How does it become a man to behave toward the American government today? I answer, that he cannot without disgrace be associated with it. I cannot for an instant recognize that political organization as my government which is the slave's government also.

How does it become a man to behave toward the American government today? I answer, that he cannot without disgrace be associated with it. I cannot for an instant recognize that political organization as my government which is the slave's government also.

Model Practice 1

Model Practice 2

Model Practice 3

CHAPTER III

Poetry from or about Early Modern History

America
by Samuel Francis Smith, (1808-1895)

My country, 'tis of thee,
Sweet land of liberty,
Of thee I sing;

Land where my fathers died,
Land of the Pilgrims' pride;
From every mountain side,
Let freedom ring.

My native country, thee—
Land of the noble free—
Thy name I love;

I love thy rocks and rills,
Thy woods and templed hills;
My heart with rapture thrills,
Like that above.

Let music swell the breeze,
And ring from all the trees
Sweet freedom's song;

Let mortal tongues awake;
Let all that breathe partake;
Let rocks their silence break—
The sound prolong.

Our fathers' God, to Thee,
Author of liberty,
To Thee we sing:

Long may our land be bright
With freedom's holy light:
Protect us by Thy might,
Great God, our King.

My native country, thee —
Land of the noble free —
Thy name I love;

I love thy rocks and rills,
Thy woods and templed hills;
My heart with rapture thrills,
Like that above.

Model Practice 1

Model Practice 2

Model Practice 3

The Anti-Slavery Alphabet

by Anonymous
1847

Listen, little children, all,
Listen to our earnest call:
You are very young, 'tis true,
But there's much that you can do.

Even you can plead with men
That they buy not slaves again,
And that those they have may be
Quickly set at liberty.

A is an Abolitionist—
A man who wants to free
The wretched slave—and give to all
An equal liberty.

B is a Brother with a skin
Of somewhat darker hue,
But in our Heavenly Father's sight,
He is as dear as you.

C is the Cotton-field, to which
This injured brother's driven,
When, as the white-man's slave, he toils,
From early morn till even.

D is the Driver, cold and stern,
Who follows, whip in hand,
To punish those who dare to rest,
Or disobey command.

E is the Eagle, soaring high;
An emblem of the free;
But while we chain our brother man,
Our type he cannot be.

F is the heart-sick Fugitive,
The slave who runs away,
And travels through the dreary night,
But hides himself by day.

A is an Abolitionist —
A man who wants to free
The wretched slave — and give to all
An equal liberty.

B is a Brother with a skin
Of somewhat darker hue,
But in our Heavenly Father's sight,
He is as dear as you.

Model Practice 1

Model Practice 2

Model Practice 3

A Book of Nonsense (excerpt)
by Edward Lear (1812-1888)

There was an Old Person of Dover,
Who rushed through a field of blue clover;
But some very large Bees stung his nose and his knees,
So he very soon went back to Dover.

There was an Old Man of the West,
Who wore a pale plum-colored vest;
When they said, "Does it fit?" he replied, "Not a bit!"
That uneasy Old Man of the West.

There was a Young Lady of Bute,
Who played on a silver-gilt flute;
She played several jigs to her Uncle's white Pigs:
That amusing Young Lady of Bute.

There was an Old Person of Mold,
Who shrank from sensations of cold;
So he purchased some muffs, some furs, and some fluffs,
And wrapped himself well from the cold.

There was an Old Lady whose folly
Induced her to sit in a holly;
Whereon, by a thorn her dress being torn,
She quickly became melancholy.

There was a Young Lady of Hull,
Who was chased by a virulent Bull;
But she seized on a spade, and called out, "Who's afraid?"
Which distracted that virulent Bull.

There was an Old Person of Dover,
Who rushed through a field of blue clover;
But some very large Bees stung his nose and his
  knees,
So he very soon went back to Dover.

There was an Old Man of the West,
Who wore a pale plum-colored vest;
When they said, "Does it fit?" he replied, "Not a
  bit!"
That uneasy Old Man of the West.

Model Practice 1

Model Practice 2

Model Practice 3

The First Thanksgiving Day
by Margaret Junkin Preston

"And now," said the Governor, gazing abroad on the piled-up store
of the sheaves that dotted the clearings and covered the meadows o'er,
"'Tis meet that we render praises because of this yield of grain;
'Tis meet that the Lord of the harvest be thanked for his sun and rain.

"And, therefore, I, William Bradford (by the grace of God today,
And the franchise of this good people), Governor of Plymouth, say,
Through virtue of vested power—ye shall gather with one accord,
And hold, in the month of November, thanksgiving unto the Lord.

"He hath granted us peace and plenty, and the quiet we've sought so long;
He hath thwarted the wily savage, and kept him from wrack and wrong;
And unto our feast the Sachem shall be bidden, that he may know
We worship his own Great Spirit, who maketh the harvests grow.

"So shoulder your matchlocks, masters—there is hunting of all degrees;
And, fishermen, take your tackle, and scour for spoils the seas;
And, maidens and dames of Plymouth, your delicate crafts employ
To honor our First Thanksgiving, and make it a feast of joy!

"We fail of the fruits and dainties—we fail of the old home cheer;
Ah, these are the lightest losses, mayhap, that befall us here;
But see, in our open clearings, how golden the melons lie;
Enrich them with sweets and spices, and give us the pumpkin-pie!"

So, bravely the preparations went on for the autumn feast;
The deer and the bear were slaughtered; wild game from the greatest to least
Was heaped in the colony cabins; brown home-brew served for wine,
And the plum and the grape of the forest, for orange and peach and pine.

At length came the day appointed; the snow had begun to fall,
But the clang from the meeting-house belfry rang merrily over all,
And summoned the folk Of Plymouth, who hastened with glad accord
To listen to Elder Brewster as he fervently thanked the Lord.

In his seat sate Governor Bradford; men, matrons, and maidens fair,
Miles Standish and all his soldiers, with corselet and sword, were there;
And sobbing and tears and gladness had each in its turn the sway,
For the grave of the sweet Rose Standish o'ershadowed Thanksgiving Day.

And when Massasoit, the Sachem, sate down with his hundred braves,
And ate of the varied riches of gardens and woods and waves,
And looked on the granaried harvest—with a blow on his brawny chest,
He muttered, "The good Great Spirit loves these pilgrims best!"

"And, therefore, I, William Bradford (by the grace of
God today,
And the franchise of this good people), Governor of
Plymouth, say,
Through virtue of vested power— ye shall gather with
one accord,
And hold, in the month of November, thanksgiving
unto the Lord.

Model Pracitce 1

Model Practice 2

Model Practice 3

Hiawatha's Childhood
by Henry W. Longfellow

By the shores of Gitche Gumee,
By the shining Big-Sea-Water,
Stood the wigwam of Nokomis,
Daughter of the Moon, Nokomis.
Dark behind it rose the forest,
Rose the black and gloomy pine-trees,
Rose the firs with cones upon them;
Bright before it beat the water,
Beat the clear and sunny water,
Beat the shining Big-Sea-Water.

There the wrinkled old Nokomis
Nursed the little Hiawatha,
Rocked him in his linden cradle,
Bedded soft in moss and rushes,
Safely bound with reindeer sinews;
Stilled his fretful wail by saying,
"Hush! the Naked Bear will hear thee!"
Lulled him into slumber, singing,
"Ewa-yea! my little owlet!
Who is this, that lights the wigwam?
With his great eyes lights the wigwam?
Ewa-yea! my little owlet!"

Many things Nokomis taught him
Of the stars that shine in heaven;
Showed him Ishkoodah, the comet,
Ishkoodah, with fiery tresses;
Showed the Death-Dance of the spirits,
Warriors with their plumes and war clubs,
Flaring far away to northward
In the frosty nights of Winter;
Showed the broad white road in heaven,
Pathway of the ghosts, the shadows,
Running straight across the heavens,
Crowded with the ghosts, the shadows.

At the door on summer evenings
Sat the little Hiawatha;
Heard the whispering of the pine-trees,
Heard the lapping of the waters,
Sounds of music, words of wonder;
"Minne-wawa!" said the Pine-trees,
"Mudway-aushka!" said the water.

Saw the fire-fly, Wah-wah-taysee,
Flitting through the dusk of evening,
With the twinkle of its candle
Lighting up the brakes and bushes,
And he sang the song of children,
Sang the song Nokomis taught him:
"Wah-wah-taysee, little fire-fly,
Little, flitting, white-fire insect,
Little, dancing, white-fire creature,
Light me with your little candle,
Ere upon my bed I lay me,
Ere in sleep I close my eyelids!"

Saw the moon rise from the water
Rippling, rounding from the water,
Saw the flecks and shadows on it,
Whispered, "What is that, Nokomis?"
And the good Nokomis answered:
"Once a warrior, very angry,
Seized his grandmother, and threw her
Up into the sky at midnight;
Right against the moon he threw her;
'T is her body that you see there."

Saw the rainbow in the heaven,
In the eastern sky, the rainbow,
Whispered, "What is that, Nokomis?"
And the good Nokomis answered:
"'T is the heaven of flowers you see there;
All the wild-flowers of the forest,
All the lilies of the prairie,
When on earth they fade and perish,
Blossom in that heaven above us."

When he heard the owls at midnight,
Hooting, laughing in the forest,
"What is that?" he cried in terror,
"What is that," he said, "Nokomis?"
And the good Nokomis answered:
"That is but the owl and owlet,
Talking in their native language,
Talking, scolding at each other."

Then the little Hiawatha
Learned of every bird its language,
Learned their names and all their secrets,
How they built their nests in Summer,
Where they hid themselves in Winter,
Talked with them whene'er he met them,
Called them "Hiawatha's Chickens."

Of all beasts he learned the language,
Learned their names and all their secrets,
How the beavers built their lodges,
Where the squirrels hid their acorns,
How the reindeer ran so swiftly,
Why the rabbit was so timid,
Talked with them whene'er he met them,
Called them "Hiawatha's Brothers."

By the shores of Gitche Gumee,
By the shining Big-Sea-Water,
Stood the wigwam of Nokomis,
Daughter of the Moon, Nokomis.
Dark behind it rose the forest,
Rose the black and gloomy pine-trees,
Rose the firs with cones upon them;
Bright before it beat the water,
Beat the clear and sunny water,
Beat the shining Big-Sea-Water.

Model Pracitce 1

Model Practice 2

Model Practice 3

The Landing of the Pilgrims
by Felicia Hemans (1793-1835)

The breaking waves dashed high
On a stern and rock-bound coast,
And the woods against a stormy sky
Their giant branches tossed.

And the heavy night hung dark
The hills and waters o'er,
When a band of exiles moored their bark
On the wild New England shore.

Not as the conqueror comes,
They, the true-hearted, came;
Not with the roll of the stirring drums,
And the trumpet that sings of fame.

Not as the flying come,
In silence and in fear;
They shook the depths of the desert gloom
With their hymns of lofty cheer.

Amid the storm they sang,
And the stars heard, and the sea,
And the sounding aisles of the dim woods rang
To the anthem of the free!

The ocean eagle soared
From his nest by the white wave's foam;
And the rocking pines of the forest roared,—
This was their welcome home!

There were men with hoary hair,
Amid that pilgrim band;
Why had they come to wither there,
Away from their childhood's land?

There was woman's fearless eye,
Lit by her deep love's truth;
There was manhood's brow serenely high,
And the fiery heart of youth.

What sought they thus afar?
Bright jewels of the mine?
The wealth of seas, the spoils of war?
They sought a faith's pure shrine!

Ay! call it holy ground,
The soil where first they trod:
They have left unstained what there they found,
Freedom to worship God.

What sought they thus afar?
Bright jewels of the mine?
The wealth of seas, the spoils of war?
They sought a faith's pure shrine!

Ay! call it holy ground,
The soil where first they trod:
They have left unstained what there they found,
Freedom to worship God.

Model Practice 1

Model Practice 2

Model Practice 3

The Little Boy Lost
by William Blake (1757-1827)

Father! Father! Where are you going?
  Oh, do not walk so fast.
Speak, father speak to your little boy,
  Or else I shall be lost.

The night was dark, no father was there;
  The child was wet with dew;
The mire was deep and the child did weep,
  And away the vapor flew.

The Little Boy Found
by William Blake (1757-1827)

The little boy lost in the lonely fen,
  Led by the wandering light,
Began to cry; but God, ever nigh,
  Appeared like his father in white;

He kissed the child, and by the hand led,
  And to his mother brought,
Who, in sorrow pale, through the lonely dale,
  Her little boy weeping sought.

The little boy lost in the lonely fen,
  Led by the wandering light,
Began to cry; but God, ever nigh,
  Appeared like his father in white;

He kissed the child, and by the hand led,
  And to his mother brought,
Who, in sorrow pale, through the lonely dale,
  Her little boy weeping sought.

Model Practice 1

Model Practice 2

Model Practice 3

Love Between Brothers and Sisters.
by Isaac Watts (1674-1748)

What ever brawls are in the street
There should be peace at home;
Where sisters dwell and brothers meet
Quarrels should never come.

Birds in their little nests agree;
And `tis a shameful sight,
When children of one family
Fall out, and chide, and fight.

Hard names at first, and threatening words,
That are but noisy breath,
May grow to clubs and naked swords,
To murder and to death.

The devil tempts one mother's son
To rage against another:
So wicked Cain was hurried on,
Till he had kill'd his brother.

The wise will make their anger cool
At least before `tis night;
But in the bosom of a fool
It burns till morning light.

Pardon, O Lord, our childish rage;
Our little brawls remove;
That as we grow to riper age,
Our hearts may all be love.

The wise will make their anger cool
At least before 'tis night;
But in the bosom of a fool
It burns till morning light.

Pardon, O Lord, our childish rage;
Our little brawls remove;
That as we grow to riper age,
Our hearts may all be love.

Model Practice 1

Model Practice 2

Model Practice 3

On a Circle
by Jonathan Swift (1667-1745)

I'm up and down, and round about,
Yet all the world can't find me out;
Though hundreds have employed their leisure,
They never yet could find my measure.
I'm found almost in every garden,
Nay, in the compass of a farthing.
There's neither chariot, coach, nor mill,
Can move an inch except I will.

On The Vowels
by Jonathan Swift (1667-1745)

We are little airy creatures,
All of different voice and features;
One of us in glass is set,
One of us you'll find in jet.
T' other you may see in tin,
And the fourth a box within.
If the fifth you should pursue,
It can never fly from you.

We are little airy creatures,
All of different voice and features;
One of us in glass is set,
One of us you'll find in jet.
T' other you may see in tin,
And the fourth a box within.
If the fifth you should pursue,
It can never fly from you.

Model Practice 1

Model Practice 2

Model Practice 3

Paul Revere's Ride
by Henry Wadsworth Longfellow (1807-1882)

Listen, my children, and you shall hear
Of the midnight ride of Paul Revere,
On the eighteenth of April, in Seventy-five;
Hardly a man is now alive
Who remembers that famous day and year.

He said to his friend, "If the British march
By land or sea from the town to-night,
Hang a lantern aloft in the belfry arch
Of the North Church tower as a signal light—
One, if by land, and two, if by sea;
And I on the opposite shore will be,
Ready to ride and spread the alarm
Through every Middlesex village and farm
For the country folk to be up and to arm,"

Then he said, "Good night!" and with muffled oar
Silently rowed to the Charlestown shore,
Just as the moon rose over the bay,
Where swinging wide at her moorings lay
The Somerset, British man-of-war;
A phantom ship, with each mast and spar
Across the moon like a prison bar,
And a huge black hulk, that was magnified
By its own reflection in the tide.

Meanwhile, his friend, through alley and street,
Wanders and watches with eager ears,
Till in the silence around him he hears
The muster of men at the barrack door,
The sound of arms, and the tramp of feet,
And the measured tread of the grenadiers,
Marching down to their boats on the shore.

Then he climbed the tower of the Old North Church,
By the wooden stairs, with stealthy tread,
To the belfry-chamber overhead,
And startled the pigeons from their perch
On the sombre rafters, that round him made
Masses and moving shapes of shade,--
By the trembling ladder, steep and tall
To the highest window in the wall,
Where he paused to listen and look down
A moment on the roofs of the town,
And the moonlight flowing over all.

Beneath, in the churchyard, lay the dead,
In their night-encampment on the hill,
Wrapped in silence so deep and still
That he could hear, like a sentinel's tread,
The watchful night-wind, as it went
Creeping along from tent to tent
And seeming to whisper, "All is well!"
A moment only he feels the spell
Of the place and the hour, and the secret dread
Of the lonely belfry and the dead;
For suddenly all his thoughts are bent
On a shadowy something far away,
Where the river widens to meet the bay,--
A line of black that bends and floats
On the rising tide, like a bridge of boats.

Meanwhile, impatient to mount and ride,
Booted and spurred, with a heavy stride
On the opposite shore walked Paul Revere.
Now he patted his horse's side,
Now gazed at the landscape far and near,
Then, impetuous, stamped the earth,
And turned and tightened his saddle-girth;
But mostly he watched with eager search
The belfry-tower of the Old North Church,
As it rose above the graves on the hill,
Lonely and spectral and sombre and still.
And lo! as he looks, on the belfry's height
A glimmer, and then a gleam of light!
He springs to the saddle, the bridle he turns,
But lingers and gazes, till full on his sight
A second lamp in the belfry burns!

A hurry of hoofs in a village street,
A shape in the moonlight, a bulk in the dark,
And beneath, from the pebbles, in passing, a spark
Struck out by a steed flying fearless and fleet:
That was all! And yet, through the gloom and the light,
The fate of a nation was riding that night;
And the spark struck out by that steed, in his flight,
Kindled the land into flame with its heat.
He has left the village and mounted the steep,
And beneath him, tranquil and broad and deep,
Is the Mystic, meeting the ocean tides;
And under the alders, that skirt its edge,
Now soft on the sand, now loud on the ledge,
Is heard the tramp of his steed as he rides.

It was twelve by the village clock

When he crossed the bridge into Medford town.
He heard the crowing of the cock,
And the barking of the farmer's dog,
And felt the damp of the river fog,
That rises after the sun goes down.

It was one by the village clock,
When he galloped into Lexington.
He saw the gilded weathercock
Swim in the moonlight as he passed,
And the meeting-house windows, blank and bare,
Gaze at him with a spectral glare,
As if they already stood aghast
At the bloody work they would look upon.

It was two by the village clock,
When he came to the bridge in Concord town.
He heard the bleating of the flock,
And the twitter of birds among the trees,
And felt the breath of the morning breeze
Blowing over the meadows brown.
And one was safe and asleep in his bed
Who at the bridge would be first to fall,
Who that day would be lying dead,
Pierced by a British musket-ball.

You know the rest. In the books you have read,
How the British Regulars fired and fled,--
How the farmers gave them ball for ball,
From behind each fence and farm-yard wall,
Chasing the red-coats down the lane,
Then crossing the fields to emerge again
Under the trees at the turn of the road,
And only pausing to fire and load.

So through the night rode Paul Revere;
And so through the night went his cry of alarm
To every Middlesex village and farm,--
A cry of defiance and not of fear,
A voice in the darkness, a knock at the door,
And a word that shall echo forevermore!
For, borne on the night-wind of the Past,
Through all our history, to the last,
In the hour of darkness and peril and need,
The people will waken and listen to hear
The hurrying hoof-beats of that steed,
And the midnight message of Paul Revere.

He said to his friend, "If the British march
By land or sea from the town tonight,
Hang a lantern aloft in the belfry arch
Of the North Church tower as a signal light—
One, if by land, and two, if by sea.

Model Practice 1 (adapted)

Model Practice 2

Model Practice 3

The Star-Spangled Banner
by Francis Scott Key (1779-1843)

Oh! say, can you see, by the dawn's early light,
  What so proudly we hailed at the twilight's last gleaming?
Whose broad stripes and bright stars through the perilous fight,
  O'er the rampart we watched, were so gallantly streaming,
And the rocket's red glare, the bombs bursting in air,
Gave proof through the night that our flag was still there,
  Oh! say, does that star-spangled banner yet wave
  O'er the land of the free and the home of the brave?

On the shore, dimly seen through the mists of the deep,
  Where the foe's haughty host in dread silence reposes,
What is that which the breeze, o'er the towering steep,
  As it fitfully blows, half conceals, half discloses?
Now it catches the gleam of the morning's first beam,
In full glory reflected now shines on the stream,
  'Tis the star-spangled banner' oh, long may it wave
  O'er the land of the free and the home of the brave!

And where is that band, who so vauntingly swore
  That the havoc of war and the battle's confusion
A home and a country should leave us no more?
  Their blood has washed out their foul footsteps' pollution.
No refuge could save the hireling and slave,
From the terror of death and the gloom of the grave,
  And the star spangled banner in triumph shall wave
  O'er the land of the free and the home of the brave!

Oh! thus be it ever, when freemen shall stand
  Between their loved homes and the war's desolation,
Blest with victory and peace, may the heaven rescued land
  Praise the power that has made and preserved us a nation.
Then conquer we must, for our cause it is just,
And this be our motto, "In God is our trust"
  And the star-spangled banner in triumph shall wave
  O'er the land of the free and the home of the brave!

*And the rocket's red glare, the bombs bursting
    in air,
Gave proof through the night that our flag
    was still there,
Oh! say, does that star-spangled banner yet
    wave
O'er the land of the free and the home of
    the brave?*

Model Practice 1

Model Practice 2

Model Practice 3

Woodman, Spare That Tree
by George P. Morris
(1802-1864)

Woodman, spare that tree!
Touch not a single bough!
In youth it sheltered me,
And I'll protect it now.
'Twas my forefather's hand
That placed it near his cot;
There, woodman, let it stand,
Thy ax shall harm it not!

That old familiar tree,
Whose glory and renown
Are spread o'er land and sea—
And wouldst thou hew it down?
Woodman, forbear thy stroke!
Cut not its earth-bound ties;
Oh! spare that aged oak,
Now towering to the skies.

When but an idle boy,
I sought its grateful shade;
In all their gushing joy
Here, too, my sisters played.
My mother kissed me here;
My father pressed my hand;
Forgive this foolish tear,
But let that old oak stand.

My heartstrings round thee cling,
Close as thy bark, old friend!
Here shall the wild bird sing,
And still thy branches bend.
Old tree! the storm still brave!
And, Woodman, leave the spot!
While I've a hand to save,
Thy ax shall harm it not.

Woodman, spare that tree!
Touch not a single bough!
In youth it sheltered me,
And I'll protect it now.
'Twas my forefather's hand
That placed it near his cot;
There, woodman, let it stand,
Thy ax shall harm it not!

Model Practice 1

Model Practice 2

Model Practice 3

CHAPTER IV

Tales from Various Cultures

A Blackfoot Story
by Edward Eggleston

Here is a story the Indians tell. It is one of the tales with which they amuse themselves in long evenings. It may be true. At least, the Indians tell it for true.

An Indian chief of the tribe called Blackfoot, or Blackfeet, went over the Rocky Mountains with a war party. He killed some of the enemies of his tribe and then started back. For fear their enemies would follow their tracks, the party did not take the usual path. They went up over the wildest part of the mountain. But when it came to going down on the other side, the Indians had a hard time.

They had to clamber over great rocks and down the sides of cliffs. Drifts of snow blocked their way in places. At last they had to stop. They stood on the edge of a cliff. Below this cliff was a ridge or shelf of rock. By tying themselves together, and so helping one another down, they reached this shelf. Below this they found still another cliff. It was harder to get down to this.

But when they had reached as far as this ledge, they were in a worse plight than ever. They stood on the brink of a great cliff. The rocks were too steep for them to get down. It was hundreds of feet to the bottom.

They tried to get back up the mountain, but that they could not do. Then they sat down and looked over the brink of the cliff. There was no chance for them to get down alive. They must stay there and starve.

The Indians filled their pipes with kinnikinnick, or willow bark, and smoked. Then they knocked the ashes out of their pipes and lay down to sleep.

But the chief did not sleep. He could not think of any way of getting out of the trouble. When morning came, they all went and looked over the cliff once more. Then they smoked again. After sitting silent for some time, the chief laid down his pipe quietly, got to his feet, and went to painting his face as if he were getting ready for a feast. He arranged his dress with the greatest care. Then he made a little speech.

"It is of no use to stay here and die," he said. "The Great Spirit is not willing that we should get away. Let us die bravely."

He added other remarks of the same kind. Then he sang his death song. When this was finished, he gave a shout, and leaped over the cliff.

When the chief had gone, the others sat down and smoked again in silence. After a long time, a weather-beaten old Indian got up and walked to the edge of the cliff.

"See," he said, "there is the soul of our chief, waiting for us to go with him to the land of spirits."

The others looked over and saw the form of a man, far below, waving the bough of a tree.

The old warrior now threw off his blanket and sang his death song. Then he leaped off. The others again looked over, and this time they saw two forms beckoning to them from below.

One after another the Indians jumped, until there were left but two young men who were little more than boys. These two boys were nephews of the chief, and they had never been in a war party.

The elder of the two showed his young brother the ghosts of the whole party standing below. He told his brother he must jump off, but the frightened boy begged to be allowed to stay and die on the bare rock.

The elder seized him, and after a struggle, pushed him over. Then he quietly gathered up all the blankets and guns and threw them off. He thought the souls of his friends would need these things in their journey to the land of spirits.

When this was done, the young man sang his own death song and jumped off. Falling swiftly as an arrow, feet downward, he struck a great snow drift at the bottom. It received him like an immense feather bed. He sank in so far that he had hard work to get out. When he had succeeded, he found all of his party, not spirits as he had expected, but living men safe and sound. The snow had saved them from injury.

Written Summation

When this was done, the young man sang his own death song and jumped off. Falling swiftly as an arrow, feet downward, he struck a great snow drift at the bottom. It received him like an immense feather bed. He sank in so far that he had hard work to get out. When he had succeeded, he found all of his party, not spirits as he had expected, but living men safe and sound. The snow had saved them from injury.

Model Practice 1

Model Practice 2

Model Practice 3

Hans, Who Made the Princess Laugh
by Peter Christen Asbjörnsen

Once upon a time there was a king who had a daughter, and she was so lovely that the reports of her beauty went far and wide. But she was so melancholy that she never laughed, and besides she was so grand and proud that she said "No" to all who came to woo her—she would not have any of them, were they ever so fine, whether they were princes or noblemen.

The king was tired of this whim of hers long ago and thought she ought to get married like other people. There was nothing she need wait for—she was old enough and she would not be any richer neither, for she was to have half the kingdom, which she inherited after her mother.

So he made known every Sunday, after the service, from the steps outside the church, that he that could make his daughter laugh should have both her and half the kingdom. But if there were any one who tried and could not make her laugh, he would have three red stripes cut out of his back and salt rubbed into them—and, sad to relate, there were many sore backs in that kingdom. Lovers from south and from north, from east and from west, came to try their luck—they thought it was an easy thing to make a princess laugh. They were a queer lot altogether, but for all their cleverness and for all the tricks and pranks they played, the princess was just as serious and immovable as ever.

But close to the palace lived a man who had three sons, and they had also heard that the king had made known that he who could make the princess laugh should have her and half the kingdom.

The eldest of the brothers wanted to try first, so away he went. And when he came to the palace, he told the king he wouldn't mind trying to make the princess laugh.

"Yes, yes! That's all very well," said the king; "but I am afraid it's of very little use, my man. There have been many here to try their luck, but my daughter is just as sad, and I am afraid it is no good trying. I do not like to see any more suffer on that account."

But the lad thought he would try anyhow. It couldn't be such a difficult thing to make a princess laugh at him, for had not everybody, both grand and simple, laughed so many a time at him when he served as soldier and went through his drill under Sergeant Nils.

So he went out on the terrace outside the princess's windows and began drilling just as if Sergeant Nils himself were there. But all in vain! The princess sat just as serious and immovable as before, and so they took him and cut three broad, red stripes out of his back and sent him home.

He had no sooner arrived home than his second brother wanted to set out and try his luck. He was a schoolmaster, and a funny figure he was altogether. He had one leg shorter than the other and limped terribly when he walked. One moment he was no bigger than a boy, but the next moment when he raised himself up on his long leg he was as big and tall as a giant—and besides he was great at preaching.

When he came to the palace and said that he wanted to make the princess laugh, the king thought that it was not so unlikely that he might.

"But I pity you, if you don't succeed," said the king, "for we cut the stripes broader and broader for every one that tries."

So the schoolmaster went out on the terrace, and took his place outside the princess's window, where he began preaching and chanting imitating seven of the parsons, and reading and singing just like seven of the clerks whom they had had in the parish.

The king laughed at the schoolmaster till he was obliged to hold on to the door post, and the princess was just on the point of smiling, but suddenly she was as sad and immovable as ever. And so it fared no better with Paul the schoolmaster than with Peter the soldier—for Peter and Paul were their names, you must know!

So they took Paul and cut three red stripes out of his back, put salt into them, and sent him home again.

Well, the youngest brother thought he would have a try next. His name was Hans. But the brothers laughed and made fun of him, and showed him their sore backs. Besides, the father would not give him leave to go, for he said it was no use his trying, who had so little sense; all he could do was to sit in a corner on the hearth, like a cat, rooting about in the ashes and cutting chips. But Hans would not give in—he begged and prayed so long, till they got tired of his whimpering, and so he got leave to go to the king's palace and try his luck.

When he arrived at the palace he did not say he had come to try to make the princess laugh, but asked if he could get a situation there. No, they had no situation for him; but Hans was not so easily put off—they might want one to carry wood and water for the kitchen maid in such a big place as that, he said. Yes, the king thought so too, and to get rid of the lad he gave him leave to remain there and carry wood and water for the kitchen maid.

One day, when he was going to fetch water from the brook, he saw a big fish in the water just under an old root of a fir tree, which the current had carried all the soil away from. He put his bucket quietly under the fish and caught it. As he was going home to the palace, he met an old woman leading a golden goose.

"Good day, grandmother!" said Hans. "That's a fine bird you have got there and such splendid feathers too! He shines a long way off. If one had such feathers, one needn't be chopping firewood."

The woman thought just as much of the fish, which Hans had in the bucket and said if Hans would give her the fish he should have the golden goose. And this goose was such that if any one touched it he would be sticking fast to it if he only said: "If you'll come along, then hang on."

Yes, Hans would willingly exchange on those terms. "A bird is as good as a fish any day," he said to himself. "If it is as you say, I might use it instead of a fishhook," he said to the woman, and felt greatly pleased with the possession of the goose.

He had not gone far before he met another old woman. When she saw the splendid golden goose, she must go and stroke it. She made herself so friendly and spoke so nicely to Hans, and asked him to let her stroke that lovely golden goose of his.

"Oh, yes!" said Hans, "but you mustn't pluck off any of its feathers!"

Just as she stroked the bird, Hans said: "If you'll come along, then hang on!"

The woman pulled and tore, but she had to hang on, whether she would or no, and Hans walked on, as if he only had the goose with him.

When he had gone some distance, he met a man who had a spite against the woman for a trick she had played upon him. When he saw that she fought so hard to get free and seemed to hang on so fast, he thought he might safely venture to pay her off for the grudge he owed her, and so he gave her a kick.

"If you'll come along, then hang on!" said Hans. And the man had to hang on and limp along on one leg, whether he would or no; and when he tried to tear himself loose, he made it still worse for himself, for he was very nearly falling on his back whenever he struggled to get free.

So on they went till they came in the neighborhood of the palace. There they met the king's smith; he was on his way to the smithy, and had a large pair of tongs in his hand. This smith was a merry fellow and was always full of mad pranks and tricks, and when he saw this procession coming jumping and limping along, he began laughing till he was bent in two, but suddenly he said:

"This must be a new flock of geese for the princess: but who can tell which is goose and which is gander? I suppose it must be the gander toddling on in front. Goosey, goosey!" he called, and pretended to be strewing corn out of his hands as when feeding geese.

But they did not stop. The woman and the man only looked in great rage at the smith for making game of them. So said the smith: "It would be great fun to see if I could stop the whole flock, many as they are!"—He was a strong man, and seized the old man with his tongs from behind in his trousers, and the man shouted and struggled hard, but Hans said:

"If you'll come along, then hang on!"

And so the smith had to hang on too. He bent his back and stuck his heels in the ground when they went up a hill and tried to get away, but it was of no use. He stuck on to the other as if he had been screwed fast in the great vise in the smithy, and whether he liked it or not, he had to dance along with the others.

When they came near the palace, the farm-dog ran against them and barked at them, as if they were a gang of tramps, and when the princess came to look out of her window to see what was the matter, and saw this procession, she burst out laughing. But Hans was not satisfied with that. "Just wait a bit, and she will laugh still louder very soon," he said, and made a tour round the palace with his followers.

When they came past the kitchen, the door was open and the cook was just boiling porridge, but when she saw Hans and his train after him, she rushed out of the door with the porridge-stick in one hand and a big ladle full of boiling porridge in the other. And she laughed till her sides shook; but when she saw the smith there as well, she thought she would have burst with laughter. When she had had a regular good laugh, she looked at the golden goose again and thought it was so lovely that she must stroke it.

"Hans, Hans!" she cried, and ran after him with the ladle in her hand; "just let me stroke that lovely bird of yours."

"Rather let her stroke me!" said the smith.

"Very well," said Hans.

But when the cook heard this, she got very angry. "What is it you say!" she cried, and gave the smith a smack with the ladle.

"If you'll come along, then hang on!" said Hans, and so she stuck fast to the others too, and for all her scolding and all her tearing and pulling, she had to limp along with them.

And when they came past the princess's window again, she was still there waiting for them, but when she saw that they had got hold of the cook too, with the ladle and porridge-stick, she laughed till the king had to hold her up. So Hans got the princess and half the kingdom, and they had a wedding which was heard of far and wide.

Written Summation

He had no sooner arrived home than his second brother wanted to set out and try his luck. He was a schoolmaster, and a funny figure he was altogether. He had one leg shorter than the other and limped terribly when he walked. One moment he was no bigger than a boy, but the next moment when he raised himself up on his long leg he was as big and tall as a giant — and besides he was great at preaching.

Model Practice 1

Model Practice 2

Model Practice 3

The Horse That Aroused the Town
by Lillian M. Gask

A wise and just monarch was the good King John. His kingdom extended over Central Italy and included the famous town of Atri, which in days gone by had been a famous harbor on the shores of the Adriatic. Now the sea had retreated from it, and it lay inland; no longer the crested waves rolled on its borders nor tossed their showers of silver spray to meet the vivid turquoise of the sky.

The great desire of good King John was that every man, woman and child in his dominions should be able to obtain justice without delay, be they rich or poor. To this end, since he could not possibly listen to all himself, he hung a bell in one of the city towers and issued a proclamation to say that when this was rung a magistrate would immediately proceed to the public square and administer justice in his name. The plan worked admirably; both rich and poor were satisfied, and since they knew that evil-doers would be quickly punished and wrongs would be set right, men hesitated to defraud or oppress their neighbors, and the great bell pealed less often as years went on.

In the course of time, however, the bell-rope wore thin, and some ingenious citizen fastened a wisp of hay to it that this might serve as a handle. One day in the height of summer, when the deserted square was blazing with sunlight, and most of the citizens were taking their noonday rest, their siesta was disturbed by the violent pealing of the bell.

"Surely some great injustice has been done," they cried, shaking off their languor and hastening to the square.

To their amazement, they found it empty of all human beings save themselves; no angry supplicant appealed for justice, but a poor old horse, lame and half blind with bones that nearly broke through his skin, was trying with pathetic eagerness to eat the wisp of hay. In struggling to do this, he had rung the bell, and the judge, summoned so hastily for so slight a cause, was stirred to indignation.

"To whom does this wretched horse belong?" he shouted wrathfully. "What business has it here?"

"Sir, he belongs to a rich nobleman, who lives in that splendid palace whose tall towers glisten white above the palm-grove," said an old man, coming forward with a deep bow.

"Time was that he bore his master to battle, carrying him dauntlessly amid shot and shell, and more than once saving his life by his courage and fleetness. When the horse became old and feeble, he was turned adrift, since his master had no further use for him; and now the poor creature picks up what food he can in highways and byways."

On hearing this, the judge's face grew dark with anger. "Bring his master before me," he thundered, and when the amazed nobleman appeared, he questioned him more sternly than he would have done the meanest peasant.

"Is it true," he demanded, "that you left this, your faithful servant, to starve, since he could no longer serve you? It is long since I heard of such gross injustice; are you not ashamed?"

The nobleman hung his head in silence; he had no word to say in his own defense as with scathing contempt the judge rebuked him, adding that in future he would neglect the horse at his peril.

"For the rest of his life," he said, "you shall care for the poor beast as he deserves, so that after his long term of faithful service he may end his days in peace."

This decision was greeted with loud applause by the town folk, who gathered in the square.

"Our bell is superior to all others," they said to each other, with nods and smiles, "for it is the means of gaining justice, not only for men but for animals too in their time of need."

And with shouts of triumph they led the old war-horse back to his stable, knowing that for the future its miserly owner would not dare to begrudge it the comfort to which it was so justly entitled.

Written Summation

To their amazement they found it empty of all human beings save themselves; no angry supplicant appealed for justice, but a poor old horse, lame and half blind with bones that nearly broke through his skin, was trying with pathetic eagerness to eat the wisp of hay. In struggling to do this, he had rung the bell, and the judge, summoned so hastily for so slight a cause, was stirred to indignation.

Model Practice 1

Model Practice 2

Model Practice 3

Mother Holle
by the Brothers Grimm

Once upon a time there was a widow who had two daughters; one of them was beautiful and industrious, the other ugly and lazy. The mother, however, loved the ugly and lazy one best because she was her own daughter. And so the other, who was only her stepdaughter, was made to do all the work of the house and was quite the Cinderella of the family. Her stepmother sent her out every day to sit by the well in the high road, there to spin until she made her fingers bleed. Now it chanced one day that some blood fell on to the spindle, and as the girl stopped over the well to wash it off, the spindle suddenly sprang out of her hand and fell into the well. She ran home crying to tell of her misfortune, but her stepmother spoke harshly to her and gave her a violent scolding.

"As you have let the spindle fall into the well you may go yourself and fetch it out," she said to her stepdaughter.

The girl went back to the well not knowing what to do, and at last in her distress she jumped into the water after the spindle.

She remembered nothing more until she awoke and found herself in a beautiful meadow, full of sunshine, and with countless flowers blooming in every direction.

She walked over the meadow, and presently she came upon a baker's oven full of bread.

"Take us out, take us out, or alas we shall be burnt to a cinder; we were baked through long ago," cried out the loaves to her.

So she took the bread-shovel and drew them all out. She went on a little farther, till she came to a tree full of apples.

"Shake me, shake me, I pray," cried the tree; "my apples, one and all, are ripe."

So she shook the tree, and the apples came falling down upon her like rain; but she continued shaking until there was not a single apple left upon it. Then she carefully gathered the apples together in a heap and walked on again.

The next thing she came to was a little house, and there she saw an old woman looking out, with such large teeth, that she was terrified and turned to run away.

But the old woman called after her, "What are you afraid of, dear child? Stay with me; if you will do the work of my house properly for me, I will make you very happy. You must be very careful, however, to make my bed in the right way, for I wish you always to shake it thoroughly, so that the feathers fly about; then they say, down there in the world, that it is snowing; for I am Mother Holle."

The old woman spoke so kindly, that the girl summoned up courage and agreed to enter into her service.

She took care to do everything according to the old woman's bidding and every time she made the bed she shook it with all her might, so that the feathers flew about like so many snowflakes. The old woman was as good as her word; she never spoke angrily to her and gave her roast and boiled meats every day.

So she stayed on with Mother Holle for some time, and then she began to grow unhappy. She could not at first tell why she felt sad, but she became conscious at last of great longing to go home; then she knew she was homesick, although she was a thousand times better off with Mother Holle than with her mother and sister.

So after waiting awhile, she went to Mother Holle and said, "I am so homesick that I cannot stay with you any longer, for although I am so happy here, I must return to my own people."

Then Mother Holle said, "I am pleased that you should want to go back to your own people, and as you have served me so well and faithfully, I will take you home myself."

Thereupon she led the girl by the hand up to a broad gateway. The gate was opened, and as the girl passed through, a shower of gold fell upon her; and the gold clung to her, so that she was covered with it from head to foot.

"That is a reward for your industry," said Mother Holle, and as she spoke she handed her the spindle which she had dropped into the well.

The gate was then closed, and the girl found herself back in the old world close to her mother's house. As she entered the courtyard, the cock who was perched on the well called out:

Cock-a-doodle-doo!
Your golden daughter's come back to you.

Then she went in to her mother and sister, and as she was so richly covered with gold, they gave her a warm welcome. She related to them all that had happened, and when the mother heard how she had come by her great riches, she thought she should like her ugly, lazy daughter to go and try her fortune. So she made the sister go, sit by the well, and spin. The girl pricked her finger and thrust her hand into a thorn-bush, so that she might drop some blood on to the spindle. Then she threw it into the well and jumped in herself.

Like her sister, she awoke in the beautiful meadow and walked over it till she came to the oven.

"Take us out, take us out, or alas! We shall be burnt to a cinder; we were baked through long ago," cried the loaves as before.

But the lazy girl answered, "Do you think I am going to dirty my hands for you?" and walked on.

Presently she came to the apple tree. 'Shake me, shake me, I pray; my apples, one and all, are ripe,' it cried. But she only answered, 'A nice thing to ask me to do, one of the apples might fall on my head,' and passed on.

At last she came to Mother Holle's house, and as she had heard all about the large teeth from her sister, she was not afraid of them and engaged herself without delay to the old woman.

The first day she was very obedient and industrious and exerted herself to please Mother Holle, for she thought of the gold she should get in return. The next day, however, she began to dawdle over her work, and the third day she was more idle still; then she began to lie in bed in the mornings and refused to get up. Worse still, she neglected to make the old woman's bed properly and forgot to shake it so that the feathers might fly about. So Mother Holle very soon got tired of her and told her she might go.

The lazy girl was delighted at this and thought to herself, "The gold will soon be mine."

Mother Holle led her, as she had led her sister, to the broad gateway; but as she was passing through, instead of the shower of gold, a great bucketful of pitch came pouring over her.

"That is in return for your services," said the old woman, and she shut the gate.

So the lazy girl had to go home covered with pitch, and the cock on the well called out as she saw her:

Cock-a-doodle-doo!
Your dirty daughter's come back to you.

But, try what she would, she could not get the pitch off and it stuck to her as long as she lived.

Written Summation

The first day she was very obedient and industrious and exerted herself to please Mother Holle, for she thought of the gold she should get in return. The next day, however, she began to dawdle over her work, and the third day she was more idle still; then she began to lie in bed in the mornings and refused to get up. Worse still, she neglected to make the old woman's bed properly and forgot to shake it so that the feathers might fly about.

Model Practice 1

Model Practice 2

Model Practice 3

The Old Man and His Grandson
by the Brothers Grimm

There was once a very old man, whose eyes had become dim, his ears dull of hearing, his knees trembled, and when he sat at table he could hardly hold the spoon and spilt the broth upon the tablecloth or let it run out of his mouth. His son and his son's wife were disgusted at this; so the old grandfather, at last, had to sit in the corner behind the stove; and they gave him his food in an earthenware bowl, and not even enough of it. And he used to look towards the table with his eyes full of tears. Once, too, his trembling hands could not hold the bowl, and it fell to the ground and broke. The young wife scolded him, but he said nothing and only sighed. Then they bought him a wooden bowl for a few halfpence, out of which he had to eat.

They were once sitting thus when the little grandson of four years old began to gather together some bits of wood upon the ground.

"What are you doing there?" asked the father.

"I am making a little trough," answered the child, "for father and mother to eat out of when I am big."

The man and his wife looked at each other for a while, and presently began to cry. Then they took the old grandfather to the table, and henceforth always let him eat with them, and likewise said nothing if he did spill a little of anything.

Written Summation

His son and his son's wife were disgusted at this; so the old grandfather, at last, had to sit in the corner behind the stove; and they gave him his food in an earthenware bowl, and not even enough of it. And he used to look towards the table with his eyes full of tears. Once, too, his trembling hands could not hold the bowl, and it fell to the ground and broke. The young wife scolded him, but he said nothing and only sighed.

Model Practice 1

Model Practice 2

Model Practice 3

Snow-White and Rose-Red
by Jacob Grimm and Wilhelm Grimm

A poor widow once lived in a little cottage. In front of the cottage was a garden, in which were growing two rose trees. One of these bore white roses and the other red.

She had two children, who resembled the rose trees. One was called Snow-White, and the other Rose-Red; and they were as religious and loving, busy and untiring, as any two children ever were.

Snow-White was more gentle and quieter than her sister, who liked better skipping about the fields, seeking flowers, and catching summer birds, while Snow-White stayed at home with her mother, either helping her in her work, or when that was done, reading aloud.

The two children had the greatest affection the one for the other. They were always seen hand in hand; and should Snow-White say to her sister, "We will never separate," the other would reply, "Not while we live," the mother adding, "That which one has, let her always share with the other."

They constantly ran together in the woods, collecting ripe berries; but not a single animal would have injured them; quite the reverse, they all felt the greatest esteem for the young creatures. The hare came to eat parsley from their hands, the deer grazed by their side, the stag bounded past them unheeding, and the birds, likewise, did not stir from the bough, but sang in entire security. No mischance befell them; if benighted in the wood, they lay down on the moss to repose and sleep till the morning; and their mother was satisfied as to their safety, and felt no fear about them.

Once, when they had spent the night in the wood, and the bright sunrise awoke them, they saw a beautiful child, in a snow-white robe, shining like diamonds, sitting close to the spot where they had reposed. She arose when they opened their eyes, and looked kindly at them; but said no word and passed from their sight into the wood. When the children looked around, they saw they had been sleeping on the edge of a precipice and would surely have fallen over if they had gone forward two steps further in the darkness. Their mother said the beautiful child must have been the angel who keeps watch over good children.

Snow-White and Rose-Red kept their mother's cottage so clean that it gave pleasure only to look in. In summertime, Rose-Red attended to the house, and every morning, before her mother awoke, she placed by her bed a bouquet, which had in it a rose from each of the rose-trees. In wintertime, Snow-White set light to the fire and put on the kettle, after polishing it until it was like gold for brightness. In the evening, when snow was falling, her mother would bid her bolt the door, and then, sitting by the hearth, the good widow would read aloud to them from a big book while the little girls were spinning. Close by them lay a lamb, and a white pigeon, with its head tucked under its wing, was on a perch behind.

One evening, as they were all sitting cozily together like this, there was a knock at the door, as if someone wished to come in.

"Make haste, Rose-Red!" said her mother; "open the door; it is surely some traveler seeking shelter."

Rose-Red accordingly pulled back the bolt, expecting to see some poor man. But it was nothing of the kind; it was a bear that thrust his big, black head in at the open door. Rose-Red cried out and sprang back, the lamb bleated, the dove fluttered her wings, and Snow-White hid herself behind her mother's bed.

The bear began speaking, and said, "Do not be afraid; I will not do you any harm; I am half-frozen and would like to warm myself a little at your fire."

"Poor bear!" the mother replied, "come in and lie by the fire; only be careful that your hair is not burnt." Then she called Snow-White and Rose-Red, telling them that the bear was kind and would not harm them. They came, as she bade them, and presently the lamb and the dove drew near also without fear.

"Children," begged the bear "knock some of the snow off my coat." So they brought the broom and brushed the bear's coat quite clean.

After that, he stretched himself out in front of the fire and pleased himself by growling a little, only to show that he was happy and comfortable. Before long, they were all quite good friends, and the children began to play with their unlooked-for visitor, pulling his thick fur, placing their feet on his back, or rolling him over and over. Then they took a slender hazel-twig, using it upon his thick coat, and they laughed when he growled. The bear permitted them to amuse themselves in this way, only occasionally calling out, when it went a little too far, "Children, spare me an inch of life."

When it was night, and all were making ready to go to bed, the widow told the bear, "You may stay here and lie by the hearth, if you like, so that you will be sheltered from the cold and from the bad weather."

The offer was accepted, but when morning came, as the day broke in the east, the two children let him out, and over the snow, he went back into the wood.

After this, every evening at the same time the bear came, lay by the fire, and allowed the children to play with him; so they became quite fond of their curious playmate, and the door was not ever bolted in the evening until he had appeared.

When springtime came and all around began to look green and bright, one morning the bear said to Snow-White, "Now I must leave you, and all the summer long I shall not be able to come back."

"Where, then, are you going, dear Bear?" asked Snow-White.

"I have to go to the woods to protect my treasure from the bad dwarfs. In wintertime, when the earth is frozen hard, they must remain underground and cannot make their way through. But now that the sunshine has thawed the earth, they can come to the surface, and whatever gets into their hands or is brought to their caves, seldom, if ever, again sees daylight."

Snow-White was very sad when she said good-bye to the good-natured beast and unfastened the door that he might go. But in going out he was caught by a hook in the lintel, and a scrap of his fur being torn, Snow-White thought there was something shining like gold through the rent. But he went out so quickly that she could not feel certain what it was, and soon he was hidden among the trees.

One day the mother sent her children into the wood to pick up sticks. They found a big tree lying on the ground. It had been felled, and towards the roots they noticed something skipping and springing, which they could not make out, as it was sometimes hidden in the grasses. As they came nearer they could see it was a dwarf with a shriveled-up face and a snow-white beard an ell long. The beard was fixed in a gash in the tree trunk; and the tiny fellow was hopping to and from, like a dog at the end of a string, but he could not manage to free himself.

He stared at the children with his red, fiery eyes, and called out, "Why are you standing there? Can't you come and try to help me?"

"What were you doing, little fellow?" inquired Rose-Red.

"Stupid, inquisitive goose!" replied the dwarf; "I meant to split the trunk, so that I could chop it up for kitchen sticks. Big logs would burn up the small quantity of food we cook, for people like us do not consume great heaps of food, as you heavy, greedy folk do. The bill-hook I had driven in, and soon I should have done what I required. But the tool suddenly sprang from the cleft, which so quickly shut up again that it caught my handsome white beard; and here I must stop, for I cannot set myself free. You stupid pale-faced creatures! You laugh, do you?"

In spite of the dwarf's bad temper, the girls took all possible pains to release the little man, but without avail, the beard could not be moved, it was wedged too tightly.

"I will run and get someone else," said Rose-Red.

"Idiot!" cried the dwarf. "Who would go and get more people? Already there are two too many. Can't you think of something better?"

"Don't be so impatient," said Snow-White. "I will try to think." She clapped her hands as if she had discovered a remedy, took out her scissors, and in a moment set the dwarf free by cutting off the end of his beard.

Immediately the dwarf felt that he was free, he seized a sack full of gold that was hidden amongst the tree's roots and, lifting it up, grumbled out, "Clumsy creatures, to cut off a bit of my beautiful beard, of which I am so proud! I leave the cuckoos to pay you for what you did." Saying this, he swung the sack across his shoulder and went off, without even casting a glance at the children.

Not long afterwards the two sisters went to angle in the brook, meaning to catch fish for dinner. As they were drawing near the water they perceived something, looking like a large grasshopper, springing towards the stream, as if it were going in. They hurried up to see what it might be, and found that it was the dwarf.

"Where are you going?" said Rose-Red. "Surely you will not jump into the water?"

"I'm not such a simpleton as that!" yelled the little man. "Don't you see that a wretch of a fish is pulling me in?"

The dwarf had been sitting angling from the side of the stream when, by ill-luck, the wind had entangled his beard in his line; and just afterwards a big fish taking the bait, the unamiable little fellow had not sufficient strength to pull it out. So the fish had the advantage and was dragging the dwarf after it. Certainly, he caught at every stalk and spray near him, but that did not assist him greatly; he was forced to follow all the twistings of the fish and was perpetually in danger of being drawn into the brook.

The girls arrived just in time. They caught hold of him firmly and endeavored to untwist his beard from the line, but in vain; they were too tightly entangled. There was nothing left but again to make use of the scissors; so they were taken out, and the tangled portion was cut off.

When the dwarf noticed what they were about, he exclaimed in a great rage, "Is this how you damage my beard? Not content with making it shorter before, you are now making it still smaller, and completely spoiling it. I shall not ever dare show my face to my friends. I wish you had missed your way before you took this road." Then he fetched a sack of pearls that lay among the rushes, and not saying another word, hobbled off, and disappeared behind a large stone.

Soon after this it chanced that the poor widow sent her children to the town to purchase cotton, needles, ribbon, and tape. The way to the town ran over a common, on which in every direction large masses of rocks were scattered about. The children's attention was soon attracted to a big bird that hovered in the air. They remarked that, after circling slowly for a time and gradually getting nearer to the ground, it all of a sudden pounced down amongst a mass of rock. Instantly a heartrending cry reached their ears, and running quickly to the place, they saw, with horror, that the eagle had seized their former acquaintance, the dwarf, and was just about to carry him off. The kind children did not hesitate for an instant. They took a firm hold of the little man and strove so stoutly with the eagle for possession of his contemplated prey, that, after much rough treatment on both sides, the dwarf was left in the hands of his brave little friends; and the eagle took to flight.

As soon as the little man had in some measure recovered from his alarm, his small squeaky, cracked voice was heard saying, "Couldn't you have held me more gently? See my little coat; you have rent and damaged it in a fine manner, you clumsy, officious things!" Then he picked up a sack of jewels and slipped out of sight behind a piece of rock.

The maidens by this time were quite used to his ungrateful, ungracious ways; so they took no notice of it but went on their way, made their purchases, and then were ready to return to their happy home.

On their way back, suddenly, once more they ran across their dwarf friend. Upon a clear space, he had turned out his sack of jewels; so that he could count and admire them; for he had not imagined that anybody would at so late an hour be coming across the common.

The setting sun was shining upon the brilliant stones, and their changing hues and sparkling rays caused the children to pause to admire them also.

"What are you gazing at?" cried the dwarf, at the same time becoming red with rage; "and what are you standing there for, making ugly faces?" It is probable that he might have proceeded in the same complimentary manner, but suddenly a great growl was heard near them, and a big black bear joined the party. Up jumped the dwarf in extreme terror, but he could not get to his hiding-place. The bear was too close to him, so he cried out in very evident anguish—

"Dear Mr. Bear, forgive me, I pray! I will render to you all my treasure. Just see those precious stones lying there! Grant me my life! What would you do with such an insignificant little fellow? You would not notice me between your teeth. See, though, those two children, they would be delicate morsels and are as plump as partridges; I beg of you to take them, good Mr. Bear, and let me go!"

But the bear would not be moved by his speeches. He gave the ill-disposed creature a blow with his paw, and he lay lifeless on the ground.

Meanwhile the maidens were running away, making off for home as well as they could; but all of a sudden, they were stopped by a well-known voice that called out, "Snow-White, Rose-Red, stay! Do not fear. I will accompany you."

The bear quickly came towards them, but as he reached their side, suddenly the bearskin slipped to the ground. And there before them was standing a handsome man, completely clothed in gold, who said, "I am a king's son, who was enchanted by the wicked dwarf lying over there. He stole my treasure, and compelled me to roam the woods transformed into a big bear until his death should set me free. Therefore he has only received a well-deserved punishment."

Some time afterwards, Snow-White married the Prince, and Rose-Red his brother.

They shared between them the enormous treasure, which the dwarf had collected in his cave.

The old mother spent many happy years with her children.

Written Summation

Rose-Red accordingly pulled back the bolt, expecting to see some poor man. But it was nothing of the kind; it was a bear that thrust his big, black head in at the open door. Rose-Red cried out and sprang back, the lamb bleated, the dove fluttered her wings, and Snow-White hid herself behind her mother's bed.

Model Practice 1

Model Practice 2

Model Practice 3

The Three Tasks
by the Brothers Grimm, from a Child's World Reader

There were once two brothers who set out to seek their fortune. They wasted their time and their money in all sorts of foolish ways, and before long they were nearly penniless.

After the two brothers had been gone some time, their younger brother, who had always been thought the simpleton of the family, set out to seek his fortune.

One day as he was passing through a village far away from home, he found his two brothers.

"Where are you going?" they asked.

"I am going to seek my fortune," he replied.

"Ha! Ha! How foolish you are!" they cried. "With all our wit and wisdom we have been unable to make our fortune. It is silly of you even to try." And they laughed and made fun of him.

Nevertheless, the three brothers decided to travel on together. As they journeyed on, they saw a large anthill by the side of the road.

The two elder brothers were about to destroy it, when the simpleton said, "Leave the poor ants alone. I will not let you disturb them."

They went on their way until they came to a pond upon which two ducks were swimming.

The two older brothers were about to kill them, when the simpleton said, "Leave them alone. I will not let you kill them."

Soon the three came to a tree in the trunk of which was a wild bee's nest. The two older brothers wished to steal the honey. They started to make a fire under the tree and smoke out the bees.

The simpleton said, "Leave the poor bees alone. I will not let you rob them."

At last the three brothers came to a castle where everything looked as if it had been turned to stone. There was not a single human being to be seen. They walked along the great wide hall, but still they saw no one.

"The castle must be enchanted," the brothers said to one another.

After passing through many rooms, they came to a door in which there were three locks. In the middle of the door was a little grating through which they could look into the room beyond.

They saw a little man, dressed in gray, seated at a table. Twice they called to him, but he did not answer. They called a third time. Then he rose, opened the three locks, and came out.

He said not a word, but led them to a table on which a feast was spread. When they had eaten and drunk as much as they wished, the old man showed each of them to a bedroom. There they rested well all night.

The next morning the little gray man came to the eldest brother and beckoned him to follow. He led him to a room in which there was a stone table, and on the table there lay three stone tablets.

On the table near the tablets was written:

"This castle is enchanted. Before the enchantment can be broken, there are three tasks to be performed. The one who performs these three tasks shall marry the youngest and dearest of the three princesses who now lie asleep in the castle."

When the eldest brother had read this, the old man gave him the first tablet. On it was written:

"In the forest, hidden beneath the thick moss, are the pearls which belonged to the princesses. They are a thousand in number. These must be collected by sunset. If one single pearl is missing, then he who has sought them shall be turned to stone."

The eldest brother searched the whole day long, but by sunset he had found only a hundred pearls. So he was turned to stone.

The following day the second brother tried his luck, but by sunset he had found but two hundred pearls. So he, too, was turned to stone.

Then it came the simpleton's turn. He searched all day amidst the moss, but he fared little better than his brothers. At last he sat down upon a stone and burst into tears.

As he sat there, the king of the ants, whose life he had once saved, came with five thousand ants. Before long the little creatures had found every one of the pearls and piled them up in a heap.

The little gray man then gave the simpleton the second tablet. Upon it was written the second task:

"The key that opens the chamber in which the princesses are sleeping lies in the bottom of the lake. He who has performed the first task must find the key."

When the simpleton came to the lake, the ducks, which he had saved, were swimming upon it. At once they dived down into the depths below and brought up the key.

The simpleton showed the key to the little gray man, who then gave him the third tablet. On it was written the third task:

"The one who has gathered the pearls and found the key to the chamber may now marry the youngest and dearest princess. He must, however, first tell which is she. The princesses are exactly alike, but there is one difference. Before they went to sleep, the eldest ate sugar, the second ate syrup, and the youngest ate honey."

The simpleton laid down the tablet with a sigh. "How can I find out which princess ate the honey?" he asked himself.

However, he put the key he had found in the lock and opened the door. In the chamber the three princesses were lying. Ah, which was the youngest?

Just then the queen of the bees flew in through the window and tasted the lips of all three. When she came to the lips that had sipped the honey, she remained there. Then the young man knew that this was the youngest and dearest princess.

So the enchantment came to an end. The sleepers awoke, and those who had been turned to stone became alive again. The simpleton married the youngest and dearest princess and was made king after her father's death. His two brothers, who were now sorry for what they had done, married the other two princesses and lived happily ever after.

Written Summation

On it was written the third task:

"The one who has gathered the pearls and found the key to the chamber may now marry the youngest and dearest princess. He must, however, first tell which is she. The princesses are exactly alike, but there is one difference. Before they went to sleep, the eldest ate sugar, the second ate syrup, and the youngest ate honey."

Model Practice 1

Model Practice 2

Model Practice 3

Why the Sea Is Salt
by Mary Howitt

There were, in very ancient times, two brothers. One of whom was rich and the other was poor. Christmas was approaching, but the poor man had nothing in the house for a Christmas dinner; so he went to his brother and asked him for a trifling gift.

The rich man was ill-natured, and when he heard his brother's request he looked very surly. But as Christmas is a time when even the worst people give gifts, he took a fine ham down from the chimney, where it was hanging to smoke, threw it at his brother, and bade him be gone and never to let him see his face again.

The poor man thanked his brother for the ham, put it under his arm, and went his way. He had to pass through a great forest on his way home. When he had reached the thickest part of it, he saw an old man, with a long, white beard, hewing timber.

"Good evening," said he to him.

"Good evening," returned the old man, raising himself up from his work and looking at him. "That is a fine ham you are carrying." On this, the poor man told him all about it.

"It is lucky for you," said the old man, "that you have met with me. If you will take that ham into the land of the dwarfs, the entrance to which lies just under the roots of this tree, you can make a capital bargain with it; for the dwarfs are very fond of ham and rarely get any. But mind what I say: you must not sell it for money, but demand for it the 'old hand mill which stands behind the door.' When you come back, I'll show you how to use it."

The poor man thanked his new friend, who showed him the door under a stone below the roots of the tree, and by this door, he entered into the land of the dwarfs. No sooner had he set his foot in it than the dwarfs swarmed about him, attracted by the smell of the ham. They offered him queer, old-fashioned money and gold and silver ore for it; but he refused all their tempting offers and said that he would sell it only for the old hand mill behind the door.

At this, the dwarfs held up their little old hands and looked quite perplexed.

"We can not make a bargain, it seems," said the poor man, "so I'll bid you all a good day."

The fragrance of the ham had by this time reached the remote parts of dwarf land. The dwarfs came flocking around in little troops, leaving their work of digging out precious ores, eager for the ham.

"Let him have the old mill," said some of the newcomers; "it is quite out of order, and he don't know how to use it. Let him have it, and we will have the ham."

So the bargain was made. The poor man took the old hand mill, which was a little thing not half so large as the ham, and went back to the woods. Here the old man showed him how to use it. All this had taken up a great deal of time, and it was midnight before he reached home.

"Where in the world have you been?" said his wife. "Here I have been waiting and waiting, and we have no wood to make a fire nor anything to put into the porridge pot for our Christmas supper."

The house was dark and cold, but the poor man bade his wife wait and see what would happen. He placed the little hand mill on the table, and began to turn the crank. First, out there came some grand, lighted wax candles, a fire on the hearth, and a porridge pot boiling over it, because in his mind he said they should come first. Then he ground out a tablecloth, and dishes, and spoons, and knives and forks.

He was himself astonished at his good luck, as you may believe, and his wife was almost beside herself with joy and astonishment. Well, they had a capital supper; and after it was eaten, they ground out of the mill every possible thing to make their house and themselves warm and comfortable. So they had a merry Christmas Eve and morning.

When the people went by the house to church, the next day, they could hardly believe their eyes. There was glass in the windows instead of a wooden shutter, and the poor man and his wife, dressed in nice new clothes, were seen devoutly kneeling in the church.

"There is something very strange in all this," said everyone.

"Something very strange indeed," said the rich man, when three days afterwards he received an invitation from his once poor brother to a grand feast.

And what a feast it was! The table was covered with a cloth as white as snow, and the dishes were all of silver or gold. The rich man could not, in his great house, and with all his wealth, set out such a table.

"Where did you get all these things?" exclaimed he.

His brother told him all about the bargain he had made with the dwarfs. And putting the mill on the table, ground out boots and shoes, coats and cloaks, stockings and gowns, and blankets. He bade his wife give them to the poor people who had all gathered about the house to get a sight of the grand feast the poor brother had made for the rich one.

The rich man was very envious of his brother's good fortune and wanted to borrow the mill, intending—for he was not an honest man—never to return it again. His brother would not lend it, for the old man with the white beard had told him never to sell or lend it to anyone.

Some years went on, and at last, the possessor of the mill built himself a grand castle on a rock by the sea, facing the west. Its windows, reflecting the golden sunset, could be seen far out from the shore. It became a noted landmark for sailors. Strangers from foreign parts often came to see this castle and the wonderful mill of which the most extraordinary tales were told.

At length, a great foreign merchant came, and when he had seen the mill, inquired whether it would grind salt. Being told that it would, he wanted to buy it; for he traded in salt, and thought that if he owned it he could supply all his customers without taking long and dangerous voyages.

The man would not sell it, of course. He was so rich now that he did not want to use it for himself; but every Christmas he ground out food and clothes and coal for the poor, and nice presents for the little children. So he rejected all the offers of the rich merchant. The merchant, however, determined to have it. He bribed one of the man's servants to let him go into the castle at night, and he stole the mill and sailed away with it in triumph.

He had scarcely got out to sea, before he determined to set the mill to work.

"Now, mill, grind salt," said the merchant. "Grind salt with all your might! Grind salt, salt, and nothing but salt!"

The mill began to grind, and the sailors began to fill the sacks. But these were soon full, and in spite of all that could be done, the salt began to fill the ship.

The dishonest merchant was now very much frightened. What was to be done? The mill would not stop grinding and at last the ship was overloaded and down it went, making a great whirlpool where it sank. The ship soon went to pieces, but the mill stands on the bottom of the sea, and keeps grinding out "salt, salt, nothing but salt!" That is the reason, say the peasants of Denmark and Norway, why the sea is salt.

Written Summation

His brother told him all about the bargain he had made with the dwarfs. And putting the mill on the table, ground out boots and shoes, coats and cloaks, stockings and gowns, and blankets. He bade his wife give them to the poor people who had all gathered about the house to get a sight of the grand feast the poor brother had made for the rich one.

Model Practice 1

Model Practice 2

Model Practice 3

APPENDIX

Models Only

For Teacher Use

Note: Paragraph-sized models from Chapters I and IV are treated as independent models and are indented.

Oral Narration Questions
(Your student may not need these questions, if he can retell the story easily.)

Questions for Chapter I, historical narratives, or Chapter IV, cultural tales.

1. Who was the main character?
2. What was the character like?
3. Where was the character?
4. What time was it in the story? Time of day? Time of year?
5. Who else was in the story?
6. Does the main character have an enemy? What is the enemy's name?
    (The enemy may also be self or nature.)
7. Does the main character want something? If not, does the main character have a problem?
8. What does the main character do? What does he say? If there are others, what do they do or say?
9. Why does the character do what he does?
10. What happens to the character as he tries to solve his problem?
11. Does the main character solve his problem? How does he solve his problem?
12. What happens at the end of the story?
13. Is there a moral to the story? If so, what was it?

Questions for Chapter II, primary source documents.
(This may be difficult for grammar stage students, help them to answer the questions. Over time, it will become easier.)

1. Who is speaking?
2. To whom is he speaking?
3. What is the main idea from the speaker?
4. Does he give facts to support his message?
5. Why is he telling this information?

Questions for Chapter III, poetry.

1. Is the poem about a character, an event, or an idea?
2. Does this poem express a feeling of happiness, sadness, anger, excitement, joy, hope, determination, or fear?
3. How does the poem make you feel?
4. Do you think the author of the poem had a message?
5. What do you think the message of the poem is?

Written Summations
(Have your student sum up the story in no more than six sentences—two for each question.)

1. What happened at the beginning of the story?
2. What happened at the middle of the story?
3. What happened at the end of the story?

Principle of Praise
Encourage, build up, praise, and celebrate your student's successes.

Let no corrupt communication
proceed out of your mouth, but
that which is good to the use of edifying,
that it may minister grace
unto the hearers.

Using the Grammar Guide

The Grammar Guide only provides an overview with definitions and a few examples of the grammar concepts. For 3rd – 5th graders, this will more than likely be enough, since the students are working with the grammar in context. But for some, this may not be enough. To supplement, you may use a separate yearlong grammar curriculum, or you, as the teacher, may purchase a guide to provide you with further explanations to pass on to your student. If you use the guide in this book, please note that the guide is not all inclusive. More advanced grammar terms, such as relative pronouns and indefinite adjectives, are not included.

1. Have your student read the model.
2. Have your student copy the selection before he marks up the model.
3. Return to the model and circle the part of speech being learned in the proper color. See page 4.
4. **For older students, have them label the parts of speech according to the definitions and abbreviations below.**
5. For adjectives, adverbs, and prepositional phrases, have your student draw an arrow to the word being modified.

Label   Definition

nouns   DO, IO, PN   direct object, indirect object, or predicate nominative

Subject is the noun that is or does something. (Who ran? What stinks?)	I ran. **The dog** stinks.
Direct objects answers what. (I ate what?)	I ate **the cookie**.
Indirect objects tell for whom the action of the verb was done.	I gave **her** the cookie.
Predicate Nominative (Noun LinkingVerb Noun.)	John is my **dad**.

verbs   AV, SB, LV   action verb, state of being, or linking verb

Action verbs with a direct object are transitive verbs.	(He kicked the ball.)
Action verbs without a direct object are intransitive.	(He kicked.)
State of being verbs are the "to be" verbs.	(am, are, is, was, were, be, being, been)
Helping verbs help the main verb express time and mood.	(do run, can clean, am eating, might hit)
Linking verbs link the subject to the predicate.	(The wind grew chilly. The wind was chilly.)
	(If I can replace grew with was, it is a LV.)

pronouns   SP, OP, PP, DP   **Subject, Object, Possessive, Demonstrative**

Subject Pronouns	I, you, he, she, it, we, they	We love to read. It was outside.
Object Pronouns	me, you, him, her, it, us, them	She took it. I handed them the candy.
Possessive Pronouns	mine, yours, his, hers, theirs, ours, its, whose	That is **mine**! Ours is blue.
Demonstrative Pronouns	this, that, these, those	**That** is mine! We love that.

adjectives   AA, PA, DA   **Attributive, Predicate, or Demonstrative Adjectives**

Attributive Adjectives modify the noun and are right next to it.	(The **big** car.)
Predicate Adjectives follow linking verbs.	(The car is **big**.)
Demonstrative Adjectives (This, that, these, those)	**That** flower grew.

adverbs   where, how, when, extent

Adverbs that tell where, how, and when modify an adverb.	(up, down, quickly, softly, yesterday, now)
Adverbs that tell extent modify an adverb or adjective.	(almost, also, only, very, enough, rather, too)

prepositions   OP   object of the preposition

GRAMMAR GUIDE
Month 1
Memorize the definitions for each part of speech. Review Weekly.
Teach the following with copywork. Circle the nouns in the copywork.

Nouns <u>**circle blue**</u>   a word that names a person, place, thing, or idea

Common nouns	**man, city, car, happiness**
Proper nouns	**David, Lake Charles, Mustang**
Subject	**Children** should appreciate their pastor.
Direct object	My parents bought **a birthday present**. (noun phrase)
Indirect object	My parents gave **the pastor** the present. (noun phrase)
Predicate Nominative	The queen is a **pilot**. (A noun that renames a noun, queen = **pilot**.)

Capitalization   Beginning of a sentence, I, proper nouns.

Month 2
Teach everything in month one and the following. Color-code the nouns and verbs in the copywork.

Verbs <u>**circle red**</u>   a word that expresses action, state of being, or links two words together

Action verbs	**jump, run, think, have, skip, throw, say, dance, smell**
State of being	any form of to be = **am, are, is, was, were, be, being, been**
Linking verbs	any "**to be**" **verb** and any verb that can logically be replaced by a "to be" verb
	She **seems** nice. She is nice. The flower **smells** stinky. The flower is stinky.
Helping verbs	am, are, is, was, were, be, being, been, do, does, did, has, have, had, may, might, must shall, will, can, should, would, could

Month 3
Teach everything previous and the following.

Pronouns <u>**circle green**</u>   a word that replaces the noun

Jack ran.	**He** ran.
Ike hit Al and Mary.	Ike hit **them**.
The car is very nice.	**That** is very nice.

Types of sentences and punctuation

Declarative or statement	I have a blue dress. The ground is wet from the rain.
Interrogative or question	Will we have dessert today? What time is it?
Imperative or demand	Come here. Sit down. Mop the floor at 2:00.
Exclamation	I sold my painting for ten million dollars!

Month 4
Teach everything previous and the following.

Adjectives <u>**circle yellow**</u>   a word that describes a noun or a pronoun
(When studying adverbs, you may have your student draw an arrow to the word being modified.)

I want candy.	I want **five** candies.	
the car	the **red** car	
I like shoes.	I like **those** shoes.	
The tall girl	The girl is **tall**.	Predicate adjectives (tall, stinky, angry)
The stinky dog	The dog smells **stinky**.	
The angry man	The man appeared **angry**.	

Month 5

Adverbs <u>circle orange</u> a word that describes a verb, another adverb, or an adjective

		Modifies the verb
Don't run.	Don't run **inside**.	tells where
The man ran.	The man ran **swiftly**.	tells how
It will rain.	It will rain **soon**.	tells when

		Modifies adjectives or other adverbs
The dog is hairy.	The dog is **very** hairy.	tells extent (modifies hairy)

Possessives words that show ownership

Mine, yours, his, hers, ours, theirs, whose	possessive pronouns (used alone)
My car, **your** house, **his** shirt, **her** computer	possessive pronouns (used with a noun)
Jane's car, Mike's shoes, Jesus' parables,	singular possessive nouns
Mom and Dad's sons, my sisters' names, children's books	plural possessive nouns

Month 6

Preposition <u>circle purple</u> a word that shows relationship between one noun and another word in the sentence
(Prepositional phrases are to be underlined)

He is **on** the box.   He is **under** the box.   He went **around** the box.   He is **in** the box.

Commas   3 items or more in a series
The elephant**,** the mouse**,** and the gnat are best friends.
I like red**,** green**,** and orange vegetables.

Month 7

Conjunction <u>circle brown</u> a word that links words, phrases, or clauses (and, but, or, nor, so, for, yet)

Jamie **and** I left.
(words)
The blue sky, the warm sun, **and** the rainbow of flowers brightened my spirits.
(phrases)
He is tall, **for** both of his parents are tall.
(independent clauses, must have a comma when combining main clauses)

Quotation Marks   Use quotation marks to set off direct quotations.

"No, I don't like peas," answered the little boy.	beginning of a sentence
The little boy answered, "I don't like peas."	end of a sentence
"No," answered the little boy, "I don't like peas."	middle of a sentence

Month 8

Interjection <u>circle black</u> a word that expresses emotion, sometimes but not always, sudden or intense.

Yes! I want ice cream too! **Well**, we're late because the car broke down.

Semi-colons   replace commas and conjunction when combining two independent clauses

My family is going to the farm**, and** we are going to have a grand time riding horses.
My family is going to the farm**;** we are going to have a grand time riding horses.

Models from Chapter I

(The first model is the same copywork model that follows that historical narrative. The second model, which is italicized, is provided for dictation. See page ix for information on studied dictation.)

Note: Paragraph sized models are treated as independent models and are indented.

from **Captain John Smith**
by Richard G. Parker

Two large stones were brought. His head was laid upon one of them, and the war clubs were raised to strike the deadly blow. At this moment, Pocahontas, the king's favorite daughter, sprang forward, threw herself between him and the executioners, and by her entreaties saved his life.

When, however, the messenger returned with the promised ransom, he regarded Smith as nothing less than a wizard and gladly allowed him to depart. It seemed to be the fate of this singular man to excite a powerful interest wherever he went.

from **A White Boy among the Indians**
by Edward Eggleston

Powhatan sent his Indians after them. They killed the Dutchman, but Henry Spelman ran away into the woods. Powhatan's men followed him, but the Potomacs reached Powhatan's men and held them back until Spelman could get away. The boy managed at last to get to the country of the Potomac Indians.

It was very lucky for Spelman that he was among the Indians at this time. Nearly all the white people in Jamestown were killed or died of hunger. Spelman lived among the Indians for years and acted as a translator between the English and the Indians.

from **The Pine-Tree Shillings**
by Nathaniel Hawthorne

Captain Hull then took a key from his girdle, unlocked the chest, and lifted its ponderous lid. Behold! It was full to the brim of bright pine-tree shillings, fresh from the mint; Samuel Sewell began to think that his father-in-law had gotten possession of all the money in the Massachusetts' treasury. But it was only the mint-master's honest share of the coinage.

Then the servants, at Captain Hull's command, heaped double handfuls of shillings into one side of the scales while Betsey remained in the other. Jingle, jingle went the shillings as handful after handful was thrown in until, plump and ponderous as she was, they fairly weighed the young lady from the floor.

from **Sir Isaac Newton**
by Nathaniel Hawthorne

He had constructed a model of the windmill. Though not so large, I suppose, as one of the box traps, which boys set to catch squirrels, yet every part of the mill and its machinery was complete. Its little sails were neatly made of linen and whirled round very swiftly when the mill was placed in a draught of air.

While the mill was at rest, he pried into its internal machinery. When its broad sails were set in motion by the wind, he watched the process by which the millstones were made to revolve and crush the grain that was put into the hopper. After gaining a thorough knowledge of its construction, he was observed to be unusually busy with his tools.

from **King Philip to the White Settler**
by Edward Everett

Stranger, the land is mine! I understand not these paper rights. I gave not my consent when, as thou sayest, these broad regions were purchased, for a few baubles, of my fathers. They could sell what was theirs; they could sell no more. How could my fathers sell that which the Great Spirit sent me into the world to live upon? They knew not what they did.

White man, there is eternal war between me and thee! I quit not the land of my fathers but with my life. In those woods, where I bent my youthful bow, I will still hunt the deer. Over yonder waters, I will still glide, unrestrained, in my bark canoe. By those dashing waterfalls, I will still lay up my winter's store of food. On these fertile meadows, I will still plant my corn.

from **King Charles II and William Penn**
by Mason L. Weems

Well, then how can I, who call myself a Christian, do what I should abhor even in the heathen? No. I will not do it. But I will buy the right of the proper owners, even of the Indians themselves. By doing this, I shall imitate God himself in his justice and mercy and, thereby, insure his blessing on my colony, if I should ever live to plant one in North America.

The right of discovery? A strange kind of right, indeed. Now suppose, friend Charles, that some canoe load of these Indians, crossing the sea and discovering this island of Great Britain, were to claim it as their own and set it up for sale over thy head, what wouldst thou think of it?

from **The Whistle**
by Benjamin Franklin

If I saw one fond of fine clothes, fine furniture, fine horses, all above his fortune, for which he contracted debts and ended his career in poverty, "Alas!" said I, "he has paid dear, very dear, for his whistle."

In short, I believed that a great part of the miseries of mankind were brought upon them by the false estimates they had made of the value of things, and by their giving too much for their whistles.

As I grew up, came into the world, and observed the actions of men, I thought I met with many, very many, who gave too much for the whistle.

When I saw any one fond of popularity, constantly employing himself in politics, neglecting his own affairs and ruining them by that neglect, "He pays, indeed," said I, "too much for his whistle."

from **Young Benjamin Franklin**
by Nathaniel Hawthorne

"My son," said Mr. Franklin solemnly, "so far as it was in your power, you have done a greater harm to the public than to the owner of the stones. I do verily believe, Benjamin, that almost all the public and private misery of mankind arises from a neglect of this great truth—that evil can produce only evil, that good ends must be wrought out by good means."

"Benjamin, come hither," began Mr. Franklin in his usual stern and weighty tone. The boy approached and stood before his father's chair. "Benjamin," said his father, "what could induce you to take property which did not belong to you?"

from **Little Lord Sold into Bondage**
by Edward Eggleston

The wicked uncle was afraid that people would find out that Jemmy was alive, so he sent a man to see where the boy was. When the boy was found, his uncle accused him of stealing a silver spoon. He hired three policemen to arrest the boy and put him on a ship. Poor Jemmy wept bitterly.

One day when he was about seventeen years old, he came into his master's house with a gun in one hand and a squirrel in the other. There were two strangers sitting by the fire. They had found the door open and had walked in.

One of the men said, "Are you a servant in this house?"

"I am," said James.

from **The Story of Peter Williamson—Twice a Slave**
by Edward Eggleston

One night, when his wife was away from home, the Indians came to his house. He got a gun and ran upstairs. He pointed the gun at the Indians, but they told him that if he did not shoot they would not kill him. So he came down and gave himself up as a prisoner.

When daylight came, he hid himself in a hollow tree. After a while, he heard the Indians running all about the tree. He could hear them tell one another how they would kill him when they found him. But they did not think to look into the tree.

from **The Intrepid Youth**
from A Sanders' Union Reader

Oh, how that mother's straining eyes followed him in his perilous career. How her heart sunk when he went under. And what a gush of joy she felt when she saw him emerging again from the waters, flinging the waves aside with his athletic arms, and struggling on in pursuit of her boy!

And, sure enough, there was the youth still unharmed and still buffeting the waters. He had just emerged from the boiling vortex below the cataract. With one hand, he held aloft the child; with the other, he was making for the shore.

from **Franklin's Wonderful Kite**
by James Baldwin

He put his knuckles close to the key, and sparks of fire came flying to his hand. He was wild with delight. The sparks of fire were electricity; he had drawn them from the clouds.

That experiment, if Franklin had only known it, was a very dangerous one. It was fortunate for him, and for the world, that he suffered no harm. More than one person who has since tried to draw electricity from the clouds has been killed by the lightning that has flashed down the hempen kite string.

from **Grandmother Bear**
by Edward Eggleston

Though they called the bear their grandmother, they made haste to take off its skin. They were glad to find that Grandma Bear was very fat. It took two persons to carry home the fat. Four more were loaded with the meat of this nice old relative of theirs.

One day Mr. Henry saw a very large pine tree that had a trunk six feet in diameter. The bark had been scratched by a bear's claws. Far up on the tree there was a large hole with small branches broken all about.

from **The Good Reader**
from   A McGuffey Eclectic Reader

His private secretary happened to be absent; and the soldier who brought the petition could not read. There was a page, or favorite boy servant, waiting in the hall and upon him the King called. The page was a son of one of the noblemen of the court, but proved to be a very poor reader.

His pronunciation was bad, and he did not modulate his voice so as to bring out the meaning of what he read. Every sentence was uttered with a dismal monotony of voice as if it did not differ in any respect from that which preceded it.

from **The Boston Tea-Party**
adapted from   John Andrews (adapted from a letter written to a friend in 1773)

That night about two hundred men, members of the Sons of Liberty dressed as Mohawk Indians, arrived on Fort Hill. They were clothed with blankets, muffled heads, and copper-colored faces. Each was armed with a hatchet or axe, and a pair of pistols.

After the tea was thrown overboard, all the Indians disappeared in a most marvelous fashion. The next day, if a stranger had walked through the streets of Boston and had seen the calm composure of the people, he would hardly have thought that ten thousand pounds of East India Company's tea had been destroyed the night before.

from **The Midnight Ride**
by   Nathaniel Hawthorne

"Well, then," said Paul Revere, "you must go back to Boston and watch. Watch, and as soon as the soldiers are ready to start, hang a lantern in the tower of the old North Church. If they are to cross the river, hang two. I will be here, ready. As soon as I see the light, I will mount my horse and ride out to give the alarm."

All at once, a light flashed out from the tower. "Ah! There it is!" he cried. The soldiers had started.
He spoke to his horse. He put his foot in the stirrup. He was ready to mount.
Then another light flashed clear and bright by the side of the first one. The soldiers would cross the river.

from **The Young Scout**
by   James Baldwin

In time, Andrew Jackson became a very great man. He was elected to Congress; he was chosen judge of the Supreme Court of Tennessee; he was appointed general in the army; and lastly he was, for eight years, the president of the United States.

The slim, tall boy seemed to grow taller as he answered, "I'll not be the servant of any Englishman that ever lived."
The captain was very angry. He drew his sword to hit the boy with its flat side. Andrew threw out his hand and received an ugly gash across the knuckles.

from **Elizabeth Zane**
by Edward Eggleston

Three or four young men offered to go. The colonel told them he could not spare more than one of them. They must settle among themselves which one should go. But each one of the brave fellows wanted to go, and none of them was willing to give up to another. Then there stepped forward a young woman named Elizabeth Zane.

But Elizabeth said, "You cannot spare a single man. There are not enough men in the fort now. If I am killed, you will be as strong to fight as before. Let the young men stay where they are needed and let me go for the powder."

from **The Capture of Major Andre**
adapted from A Sanders' Union Reader

Arnold lived; but with the thirty thousand dollars—the price of his treachery—he lived a miserable man, despised even by those who bought him. And one impressive lesson, which the story teaches, is that the consequences of guilt do not fall alone on the guilty man; others are often involved in distress, disgrace, and ruin.

Andre told them he had a pass to White Plains on urgent business from General Arnold and begged them not to detain him; but the men, suspecting that all was not right, began to search him; and hauling off his boots, they discovered his papers in his stockings.

from **Webster and the Woodchuck**
adapted from A Sanders' Union Reader (adapted from Boston Traveler)

During this appeal, the tears had started to the old man's eyes and were fast running down his sunburned cheeks. Every feeling of a father's heart was stirred within him. He saw the future greatness of his son before his eyes and felt that God had blessed him in his children, beyond the lot of most men.

"God," he said, "has made the woodchuck; he made him to live, to enjoy the bright sunlight, the pure air, the free fields and woods. God has not made him, or anything, in vain; the woodchuck has as much right to life as any other living thing."

from **Benedict Arnold**
from A Sanders' Union Reader

There was a day when Talleyrand arrived in Havre, direct from Paris. It was the darkest hour of the French Revolution. Pursued by the bloodhounds of the Reign of Terror, stripped of every wreck of property or power, Talleyrand secured a passage to America aboard a ship about to sail. He was a beggar and a wanderer in a strange land, looking to earn his bread by daily labor.

The strange gentleman rose. With a look that Talleyrand never forgot, he retreated to the door of the next chamber, his eyes looking still from beneath his darkened brow. He spoke as he retreated backward; his voice was full of meaning.

from **Old Johnny Appleseed**
by Elizabeth Harrison

In the springtime the young men gathered the blossoms for the young maidens to wear in their hair, and in the autumn the fathers gathered the ripe red and yellow apples to store away in their cellars for winter use. The mothers made applesauce and apple pies and apple dumplings of them, and all the year round the little children played under the shade of the apple trees.

When the cold winters came and the ground was frozen too hard for him to plant his apple seeds, he still saved them and would often have a small bag full of them by the time that spring returned again. And this is how he came to be called "Old Johnny Appleseed."

from **Napoleon's Army Crossing the Alps**
from A Sanders' Union Reader

When halfway up the summit, a rumbling noise was heard among the cliffs. The guides looked at each other in alarm for they knew well what it meant. It grew louder and louder. "An avalanche! An avalanche!" they shrieked, and the next moment a field of ice and snow came leaping down the mountain, striking the line of march, and sweeping thirty dragoons in a wild plunge below.

When Napoleon was carrying war into Italy, he ordered one of his officers, Marshal Macdonald, to cross the Splugen with fifteen thousand soldiers and join him on the plains below. The Splugen is one of the four great roads which cross the Alps from Switzerland to Italy.

from **A Foot Race for Life**
by Edward Eggleston

He almost flew over the ground. At first he did not turn his head round; however, when he had run about three miles, he glanced back. He saw that most of the Indians had lost ground, but the best runners were ahead of the others. One Indian, swifter than all the rest, was only about a hundred yards behind him. This man had a spear in his hand, ready to kill Colter as soon as he should be near enough.

The Indian was surprised at this. He tried to stop running, so as to kill the white man with his spear. But he had already run himself nearly to death, and when he tried to stop quickly, he lost his balance and fell forward to the ground. His lance stuck in the earth and broke in two.

from **The Rescue**
adapted from A Sanders' Union Reader (by a Sea Captain)

Such a pull! We bent forward until our faces almost touched our knees; and then throwing all our strength into the backward movement, drew on the oar until every inch covered by the sweep was gained. Thus we worked at the oars for fifteen minutes, and it seemed to me as many hours. The sweat rolled off in great drops, and I was enveloped in a steam generated from my own body.

I kept my eye upon the receding mass of ice, while the moon was slowly working her way through a heavy bank of clouds. The mate stood by me with the glass. And when the full light fell upon the water, with brilliance only known in our northern latitudes, I put the glass to my eye. One glance was enough.

from **The Whisperers**
by James Baldwin

The children thought the new game was very funny. First, Tommy Jones whispered to Billy Brown and was at once called out to stand on the floor. Within less than two minutes, Billy saw Mary Green whispering, and she had to take his place. Mary looked around and saw Samuel Miller asking his neighbor for a pencil, and Samuel was called.

"I did it to save little Lucy," said the awkward boy, standing up very straight and brave. "I could not bear to see her punished."
"Elihu, you may go home," said the master.

from **Finding Gold in California**
by Edward Eggleston

When the Indians had partly dug this ditch, Marshall went out one January morning to look at it. The clear water was running through the ditch. It had washed away the sand, leaving the pebble exposed. At the bottom of the water Marshall saw the pebble which looked like brass. He put his hand down into the water and took up this bright, yellow pebble.

Marshall knew that if it were gold it would not break easily. He laid one of the pieces on a stone; then he took another stone and hammered it. It was soft and did not break. If it had broken to pieces, Marshall would have known that it was not gold.

Models from Chapter II

from **The Mayflower Compact**

Having undertaken for the Glory of God, and Advancement of the Christian Faith, and the Honor of our King and Country, a Voyage to plant the first colony in the Northern Parts of Virginia; do, by these Presents, solemnly and mutually in the Presence of God and one of another, covenant and combine ourselves together into a civil Body Politick, for our better Ordering and Preservation, and Furtherance of the Ends aforesaid.

from **Benjamin Franklin's 13 Virtues**
from Benjamin Franklin's autobiography

1. Temperance: Eat not to dullness; drink not to elevation.
2. Silence: Speak not but what may benefit others or yourself; avoid trifling conversation.
3. Order: Let all your things have their places; let each part of your business have its time.
4. Resolution: Resolve to perform what you ought; perform without fail what you resolve.
5. Frugality: Make no expense but to do good to others or yourself; i.e., waste nothing.

8. JUSTICE. *Wrong none by doing injuries, or omitting the benefits that are your duty.*
9. MODERATION. *Avoid extremes; forbear resenting injuries so much as you think they deserve.*
10. CLEANLINESS. *Tolerate no uncleanliness in body, cloths, or habitation.*
11. TRANQUILLITY. *Be not disturbed at trifles, or at accidents common or unavoidable.*

from **Give Me Liberty or Give Me Death**
by Patrick Henry

Our brethren are already in the field! Why stand we here idle? What is it that gentlemen wish? What would they have? Is life so dear, or peace so sweet, as to be purchased at the price of chains and slavery? Forbid it, Almighty God! I know not what course others may take; but as for me, give me liberty or give me death!

Besides, sir, we shall not fight our battles alone. There is a just God who presides over the destinies of nations, and who will raise up friends to fight our battles for us. The battle, sir, is not to the strong alone; it is to the vigilant, the active, the brave.

from **Common Sense**
by Thomas Paine

With the increase of commerce, England hath lost its spirit. The city of London, notwithstanding its numbers, submits to continued insults with the patience of a coward. The more men have to lose, the less willing are they to venture. The rich are in general slaves to fear, and submit to courtly power with the trembling duplicity of a Spaniel.

Perhaps the sentiments contained in the following pages, are not yet sufficiently fashionable to procure them general favor; a long habit of not thinking a thing wrong gives it a superficial appearance of being right and raises at first a formidable outcry in defense of custom. But tumult soon subsides. Time makes more converts than reason.

from **The Declaration of Independence**

When in the Course of human events, it becomes necessary for one people to dissolve the political bands which have connected them with another, and to assume, among the Powers of the earth, the separate and equal station to which the Laws of Nature and of Nature's God entitle them, a decent respect to the opinions of mankind requires that they should declare the causes which impel them to the separation.

Perhaps the sentiments contained in the following pages, are not yet sufficiently fashionable to procure them general favor; a long habit of not thinking a thing wrong gives it a superficial appearance of being right and raises at first a formidable outcry in defense of custom. But tumult soon subsides. Time makes more converts than reason.

Preamble to The Constitution

We the people of the United States, in Order to form a more perfect Union, establish Justice, insure domestic Tranquility, provide for the common defense, promote the general Welfare, and secure the Blessings of Liberty to ourselves and our Posterity, do ordain and establish this Constitution for the United States of America.

5. Every citizen is guaranteed a speedy trial by jury.
6. Congress cannot pass a law to punish a crime already committed.
7. Bills of revenue can originate only in the House of Representatives.
8. A person committing a crime in one State cannot find refuge in another.

from **A letter to James Madison**
by Thomas Jefferson

I will now tell you what I do not like. First, the omission of a bill of rights, providing clearly, and without the aid of sophism, for freedom of religion, freedom of the press, protection against standing armies, restriction of monopolies, the eternal and unremitting force of the habeas corpus laws, and trials by jury in all matters of fact triable by the laws of the land, and not by the laws of nations.

I like much the general idea of framing a government which should go on of itself, peaceably, without needing continual recurrence to the State legislatures. I like the organization of the government into legislative, judiciary, and executive. I like the power given the legislature to levy taxes, and for that reason solely, I approve of the greater House being chosen by the people directly.

from **The United States Bill of Rights**

Congress shall make no law respecting an establishment of religion, or prohibiting the free exercise thereof; or abridging the freedom of speech, or of the press, or the right of the people peaceably to assemble, and to petition the Government for a redress of grievances.

IX
The enumeration in the Constitution, of certain rights, shall not be construed to deny or disparage others retained by the people.

X
The powers not delegated to the United States by the Constitution, nor prohibited by it to the States, are reserved to the States respectively, or to the people.

from **Proclamation of A National Thanksgiving**
by George Washington

Now, therefore, I do recommend and assign Thursday, the 26th day of November next, to be devoted by the people of these States to the service of that great and glorious Being who is the beneficent author of all the good that was, that is, or that will be; that we may then all unite in rendering unto Him our sincere and humble thanks for His kind care and protection of the people of this country previous to their becoming a nation.

And also that we may then unite in most humbly offering our prayers and supplications to the great Lord and Ruler of Nations and beseech Him to pardon our national and other transgressions. (adapted)

from **George Washington's Farewell Address**
by George Washington

The period for a new election of a citizen to administer the Executive Government of the United States being not far distant, and the time actually arrived when your thoughts must be employed in designating the person who is to be clothed with that important trust, it appears to me proper, especially as it may conduce to a more distinct expression of the public voice, that I should now apprise you of the resolution I have formed to decline being considered among the number of those out of whom a choice is to be made.

Though in reviewing the incidents of my Administration I am unconscious of intentional error; I am, nevertheless, too sensible of my defects not to think it probable that I may have committed many errors. Whatever they may be, I fervently beseech the Almighty to avert or mitigate the evils to which they may tend.

from **Jefferson's Letter to the Danbury Baptists**
by Thomas Jefferson

Believing with you that religion is a matter which lies solely between Man and his God, that he owes account to none other for his faith or his worship, that the legitimate powers of government reach actions only and not opinions, I contemplate with sovereign reverence that act of the whole American people which declared that their legislature should "make no law respecting an establishment of religion, or prohibiting the free exercise thereof," thus building a wall of separation between Church and State.

Adhering to this expression of the supreme will of the nation in behalf of the rights of conscience, I shall see with sincere satisfaction the progress of those sentiments which tend to restore to man all his natural rights, convinced he has no natural right in opposition to his social duties.

from President Andrew Jackson on Indian Removal

Rightly considered, the policy of the General Government toward the red man is not only liberal, but generous. He is unwilling to submit to the laws of the States and mingle with their population. To save him from this alternative, or perhaps utter annihilation, the General Government kindly offers him a new home, and proposes to pay the whole expense of his removal and settlement.

The present policy of the Government is but a continuation of the same progressive change by a milder process. The tribes which occupied the countries now constituting the Eastern States were annihilated or have melted away to make room for the whites.

from Life of Tecumseh
by Benjamin Drake

He was, says an intelligent Shawanoe, who had known him from childhood, kind and attentive to the aged and infirm, looking personally to their comfort, repairing their frail wigwams when winter approached, giving them skins for moccasins and clothing, and sharing with them the choicest game which the woods and the seasons afforded. Nor were these acts of kindness bestowed exclusively on those of rank or reputation.

"From the earliest period of his life," says Mr. Johnston, the late Indian agent at Piqua, "Tecumseh was distinguished for virtue, for a strict adherence to truth, honor, and integrity. He was sober and abstemious, never indulging in the use of liquor nor eating to excess."

from Life and Adventures of Black Hawk
by George Conclin

Here he had a very comfortable bark cabin, which he furnished in imitation of the whites, with chairs, a table, a mirror, and mattrasses. His dress was that of the other chiefs, with the exception of a broad-brimmed black hat, which he usually wore. In the summer he cultivated a few acres of land in corn, melons, and various kinds of vegetables. He was frequently visited by the whites, and I have often heard his hospitality highly commended.

It has pleased the Great Spirit that I am here today. I have eaten with my white friends. The earth is our mother. We are now on it, with the Great Spirit above us. It is good. I hope we are all friends here. A few winters ago, I was fighting against you. I did wrong, perhaps; but that is past. It is buried. Let it be forgotten.

from A Slave Narrative
by Henry Bibb

Or, more correctly speaking, in the above counties, I may safely say, I was flogged up; for where I should have received moral, mental, and religious instruction, I received stripes without number, the object of which was to degrade and keep me in subordination. I can truly say, that I drank deeply of the bitter cup of suffering and woe. I have been dragged down to the lowest depths of human degradation and wretchedness, by Slaveholders.

The first time I was separated from my mother, Mildred Jackson, I was young and small. I knew nothing of my condition then as a slave. I was living with Mr. White, whose wife had died and left him a widower with one little girl, who was said to be the legitimate owner of my mother and all her children. This girl was also my playmate when we were children. (adapted)

from **On the Duty of Civil Disobedience**
    by Henry David Thoreau

How does it become a man to behave toward the American government today? I answer, that he cannot without disgrace be associated with it. I cannot for an instant recognize that political organization as my government which is the slave's government also.

The objections which have been brought against a standing army, and they are many and weighty and deserve to prevail, may also at last be brought against a standing government. The standing army is only an arm of the standing government. The government itself, which is only the mode which the people have chosen to execute their will, is equally liable to be abused and perverted before the people can act through it.

Models from Chapter III

from **America**
by Samuel Francis Smith

My native country, thee—
Land of the noble free—
Thy name I love;

I love thy rocks and rills,
Thy woods and templed hills;
My heart with rapture thrills,
Like that above.

My country, 'tis of thee,
Sweet land of liberty,
Of thee I sing;

Land where my fathers died,
Land of the Pilgrims' pride;
From every mountain side,
Let freedom ring.

from **The Anti-Slavery Alphabet**
by Anonymous

A is an Abolitionist—
A man who wants to free
The wretched slave—and give to all
An equal liberty.

B is a Brother with a skin
Of somewhat darker hue,
But in our Heavenly Father's sight,
He is as dear as you.

E is the Eagle, soaring high;
An emblem of the free;
But while we chain our brother man,
Our type he cannot be.

F is the heart-sick Fugitive,
The slave who runs away,
And travels through the dreary night,
But hides himself by day.

from **A Book of Nonsense**
by Edward Lear

There was an Old Person of Dover,
Who rushed through a field of blue clover;
But some very large Bees stung his nose and his knees,
So he very soon went back to Dover.

There was an Old Man of the West,
Who wore a pale plum-colored vest;
When they said, "Does it fit?" he replied, "Not a bit!"
That uneasy Old Man of the West.

There was an Old Person of Mold,
Who shrank from sensations of cold;
So he purchased some muffs, some furs, and some fluffs,
And wrapped himself well from the cold.

There was an Old Lady whose folly
Induced her to sit in a holly;
Whereon, by a thorn her dress being torn,
She quickly became melancholy.

from **The First Thanksgiving Day**
by Margaret Junkin Preston

"And, therefore, I, William Bradford (by the grace of God today,
And the franchise of this good people), Governor of Plymouth, say,
Through virtue of vested power ye shall gather with one accord,
And hold, in the month of November, thanksgiving unto the Lord.

So, bravely the preparations went on for the autumn feast;
The deer and the bear were slaughtered; wild game from the greatest to least
Was heaped in the colony cabins; brown home-brew served for wine,
And the plum and the grape of the forest, for orange and peach and pine.

from **Hiawatha's Childhood**
by Henry W. Longfellow

By the shores of Gitche Gumee,
By the shining Big-Sea-Water,
Stood the wigwam of Nokomis,
Daughter of the Moon, Nokomis.
Dark behind it rose the forest,
Rose the black and gloomy pine-trees,
Rose the firs with cones upon them;
Bright before it beat the water,
Beat the clear and sunny water,
Beat the shining Big-Sea-Water.

At the door on summer evenings
Sat the little Hiawatha;
Heard the whispering of the pine-trees,
Heard the lapping of the waters,
Sounds of music, words of wonder;
"Minne-wawa!" said the Pine-trees,
"Mudway-aushka!" said the water.

from **The Landing of the Pilgrims**
by Felicia Hemans

What sought they thus afar?
Bright jewels of the mine?
The wealth of seas, the spoils of war?
They sought a faith's pure shrine!

Ay! call it holy ground,
The soil where first they trod:
They have left unstained what there they found,
Freedom to worship God.

Amid the storm they sang,
And the stars heard, and the sea,
And the sounding aisles of the dim woods rang
To the anthem of the free!

The ocean eagle soared
From his nest by the white wave's foam;
And the rocking pines of the forest roared,—
This was their welcome home!

The Little Boy Found
by William Blake

The little boy lost in the lonely fen,
  Led by the wandering light,
Began to cry; but God, ever nigh,
  Appeared like his father in white;

He kissed the child, and by the hand led,
  And to his mother brought,
Who, in sorrow pale, through the lonely dale,
  Her little boy weeping sought.

Father! Father! Where are you going?
  Oh, do not walk so fast.
Speak, father speak to your little boy,
  Or else I shall be lost.

The night was dark, no father was there;
  The child was wet with dew;
The mire was deep and the child did weep,
  And away the vapor flew.

from Love Between Brothers and Sisters
by Isaac Watts

The wise will make their anger cool
At least before 'tis night;
But in the bosom of a fool
It burns till morning light.

Pardon, O Lord, our childish rage;
Our little brawls remove;
That as we grow to riper age,
Our hearts may all be love.

Whatever brawls are in the street
There should be peace at home;
Where sisters dwell and brothers meet
Quarrels should never come.

Birds in their little nests agree;
And 'tis a shameful sight,
When children of one family
Fall out, and chide, and fight.

On the Circle / Vowels
    by   Jonathan Swift

We are little airy creatures,
All of different voice and features;
One of us in glass is set,
One of us you'll find in jet.
T' other you may see in tin,
And the fourth a box within.
If the fifth you should pursue,
It can never fly from you.

I'm up and down, and round about,
Yet all the world can't find me out;
Though hundreds have employed their leisure,
They never yet could find my measure.
I'm found almost in every garden,
Nay, in the compass of a farthing.
There's neither chariot, coach, nor mill,
Can move an inch except I will.

from Paul Revere's Ride
    by   Henry Wadsworth Longfellow

He said to his friend, "If the British march
By land or sea from the town tonight,
Hang a lantern aloft in the belfry arch
Of the North Church tower as a signal light—
One, if by land, and two, if by sea.

And I on the opposite shore will be,
Ready to ride and spread the alarm
Through every Middlesex village and farm
For the country folk to be up and to arm,"

from The Star-Spangled Banner
    by   Francis Scott Key

And the rocket's red glare, the bombs bursting in air,
Gave proof through the night that our flag was still there,
  Oh! say, does that star-spangled banner yet wave
  O'er the land of the free and the home of the brave?

Oh! say, can you see, by the dawn's early light,
  What so proudly we hailed at the twilight's last gleaming?
Whose broad stripes and bright stars through the perilous fight,
  O'er the rampart we watched, were so gallantly streaming,

from **Woodman, Spare That Tree**
by George P. Morris

Woodman, spare that tree!
Touch not a single bough!
In youth it sheltered me,
And I'll protect it now.
'Twas my forefather's hand
That placed it near his cot;
There, woodman, let it stand,
Thy ax shall harm it not!

When but an idle boy,
I sought its grateful shade;
In all their gushing joy
Here, too, my sisters played.
My mother kissed me here;
My father pressed my hand;
Forgive this foolish tear,
But let that old oak stand.

Models from Chapter IV

from **A Blackfoot Story**
by Edward Eggleston

When this was done, the young man sang his own death song and jumped off. Falling swiftly as an arrow, feet downward, he struck a great snow drift at the bottom. It received him like an immense feather bed. He sank in so far that he had hard work to get out. When he had succeeded, he found all of his party, not spirits as he had expected, but living men safe and sound. The snow had saved them from injury.

When the chief had gone, the others sat down and smoked again in silence. After a long time, a weather beaten old Indian got up and walked to the edge of the cliff.

"See," he said, "there is the soul of our chief, waiting for us to go with him to the land of spirits."

from **Hans, Who Made the Princess Laugh**
by Peter Christen Asbjörnsen

He had no sooner arrived home than his second brother wanted to set out and try his luck. He was a schoolmaster, and a funny figure he was altogether. He had one leg shorter than the other and limped terribly when he walked. One moment he was no bigger than a boy, but the next moment when he raised himself up on his long leg he was as big and tall as a giant—and besides he was great at preaching.

When he had gone some distance, he met a man who had a spite against the woman for a trick she had played upon him. When he saw that she fought so hard to get free and seemed to hang on so fast, he thought he might safely venture to pay her off for the grudge he owed her, and so he gave her a kick.

from **The Horse That Aroused the Town**
by Lillian M. Gask

To their amazement, they found it empty of all human beings save themselves; no angry supplicant appealed for justice, but a poor old horse, lame and half blind with bones that nearly broke through his skin, was trying with pathetic eagerness to eat the wisp of hay. In struggling to do this, he had rung the bell, and the judge, summoned so hastily for so slight a cause, was stirred to indignation.

The nobleman hung his head in silence. He had no word to say in his own defense as with scathing contempt the judge rebuked him, adding that in future he would neglect the horse at his peril.

from **Mother Holle**
by The Brothers Grimm

The first day she was very obedient and industrious and exerted herself to please Mother Holle, for she thought of the gold she should get in return. The next day, however, she began to dawdle over her work, and the third day she was more idle still; then she began to lie in bed in the mornings and refused to get up. Worse still, she neglected to make the old woman's bed properly and forgot to shake it so that the feathers might fly about.

She took care to do everything according to the old woman's bidding and every time she made the bed, she shook it with all her might, so that the feathers flew about like so many snowflakes. The old woman was as good as her word; she never spoke angrily to her and gave her roast and boiled meats every day.

from **The Old Man and His Grandson**
by The Brothers Grimm

His son and his son's wife were disgusted at this; so the old grandfather, at last, had to sit in the corner behind the stove; and they gave him his food in an earthenware bowl, and not even enough of it. And he used to look towards the table with his eyes full of tears. Once, too, his trembling hands could not hold the bowl, and it fell to the ground and broke. The young wife scolded him, but he said nothing and only sighed.

They were once sitting thus, when the little grandson of four years old began to gather some bits of wood upon the ground.
"What are you doing there?" asked the father.
"I am making a little trough," answered the child, "for father and mother to eat out of when I am big."

from **Snow-White and Rose-Red**
by Jacob Grimm and Wilhelm Grimm

Rose-Red accordingly pulled back the bolt, expecting to see some poor man. But it was nothing of the kind; it was a bear that thrust his big, black head in at the open door. Rose-Red cried out and sprang back, the lamb bleated, the dove fluttered her wings, and Snow-White hid herself behind her mother's bed.

"Don't be so impatient," said Snow-White. "I will try to think." She clapped her hands as if she had discovered a remedy, took out her scissors, and in a moment set the dwarf free by cutting off the end of his beard.

from **The Three Tasks**
   by   The Brothers Grimm
On it was written the third task:

"The one who has gathered the pearls and found the key to the chamber may now marry the youngest and dearest princess. He must, however, first tell which is she. The princesses are exactly alike, but there is one difference. Before they went to sleep, the eldest ate sugar, the second ate syrup, and the youngest ate honey."

Soon the three came to a tree in the trunk of which was a wild bee's nest. The two older brothers wished to steal the honey. They started to make a fire under the tree and smoke out the bees.
The simpleton said, "Leave the poor bees alone. I will not let you rob them."

from **Why the Sea Is Salt**
   by   Mary Howitt
His brother told him all about the bargain he had made with the dwarfs. And putting the mill on the table, ground out boots and shoes, coats and cloaks, stockings and gowns, and blankets. He bade his wife give them to the poor people who had all gathered about the house to get a sight of the grand feast the poor brother had made for the rich one.

When the people went by the house to church the next day, they could hardly believe their eyes. There was glass in the windows instead of a wooden shutter, and the poor man and his wife, dressed in nice new clothes, were seen devoutly kneeling in the church.
"There is something very strange in all this," said everyone.

Made in the USA
Middletown, DE
24 October 2020